Blender 2.8

The beginner's guide

Allan Brito

Description and data

Technical info about the Book

Author: Allan Brito

Reference: blender3darchitect.com

Edition: 1st

Cover image credits: Alvaro Pinot @Unsplash

Licensed in public domain - https://unsplash.com/license

Blender version used in the Book: 2.80 and *2.81 alpha*

First edition date: September 2019

ISBN: 9781694960498

Imprint: Independently published

About the author

Allan Brito is a Brazilian architect that has a passion for applying technology and open source to design and visualization. He is a longtime Blender user ever since 2005, and believes the software can become a great player in the architecture and design markets.

You will find more about him and the use of Blender for architecture in **blender3darchitect.com**, where he writes articles about the subject on a daily basis.

Who should read this book?

The book has a goal of guiding artists looking to start using Blender 2.8. No matter if you already know Blender. We will start from the very beginning. If you are planning to use Blender 2.8 to create 3D models, animations, and overall rendering this book you help you start from scratch.

You don't need any previous experience with Blender to follow the chapters.

Foreword

Across the years you will find artists looking at Blender with some doubts about the reliability and also ease of use. The interface and overall usability always pushed people away from Blender and until recently was one of the biggest complaints from people trying to use the software for the first time.

The release of Blender 2.8 came to change everything you think you know about Blender. We now have a revamped user interface that is incredibly easy to use, and an incredible set of tools for content production.

With a friendly user interface for beginners and options to render in real-time, you will find in Blender 2.8 a powerful ally to produce content. You can use the software to work on:

- Architectural visualization

- Animations

- Characters

- Product design

- Game development

- Advertisement media

- Visual FX

Our purpose with The beginner's guide for Blender 2.8 is to give you a detailed explanation about how the software works, from an inexperienced artist.

We will start with the basics for the user interface and go to 3D modeling, rendering, and animation. Even if you are trying to migrate from older versions of Blender, you will find the guide useful to show you will the most important aspects of Blender 2.8.

I hope you find the content useful, and by the end of the book, you feel more comfortable to use Blender for all your projects!

Allan Brito

Downloading Blender

One of the significant advantages of Blender when comparing to similar softwares is their open source nature. You can use Blender without any hidden costs! All you have to do is download the software and start using it.

How to download it? To download Blender, you should visit the Blender Foundation website:

https://www.blender.org/download/

For this book, we will use version *2.80 of Blender*, but the vast majority of techniques will still work with later versions.

Intentionally left blank

TABLE OF CONTENTS

Chapter 1 - Blender user interface and 3D navigation

The first chapter of our guide for Blended 2.8 will focus on core concepts regarding the user interface and the overall use of Blender. You will learn how to manage the selection and other aspects of the software.

You will learn about active editors and the use of keyboard shortcuts to speed up any project in Blender. That is an important chapter because it will create a solid base for the rest of our guide. If you don't have any previous experience with Blender, you must read and practice all recommendations from this chapter.

Here is a list of what you will learn:

- Handling object selection

- Working with the user interface

- Choosing and changing editors

- Using keyboard shortcuts and active editors

- Working with the 3D Cursor and the Snap

- Moving and placing objects based on the 3D Cursor

- 3D Navigation and zoom shortcuts

1.1 First time with Blender

After you download and install Blender in your computer, you will open the software and see a quick set-up screen that will ask a few critical questions. The most crucial choice you have to make in this screen is how you want to handle object selection.

In the past, Blender used the right mouse button to select objects, which is the opposite of all other graphical applications. Starting with Blender 2.8, the new default behavior is to use the left mouse button for selection.

You can confirm in the Quick Setup that you will use the left button for selection. For the rest of the book, I will assume you choose the "Left" option (*Select With*) from the Quick Setup (Figure 1.1).

Figure 1.1 - *Blender Quick Setup*

You can always change those settings later in Blender using the **Edit** → **User Preferences** menu. To modify your selection, use the Keymap tab in the preferences, which will allow you to swap between the left or right mouse buttons for selection (Figure 1.2).

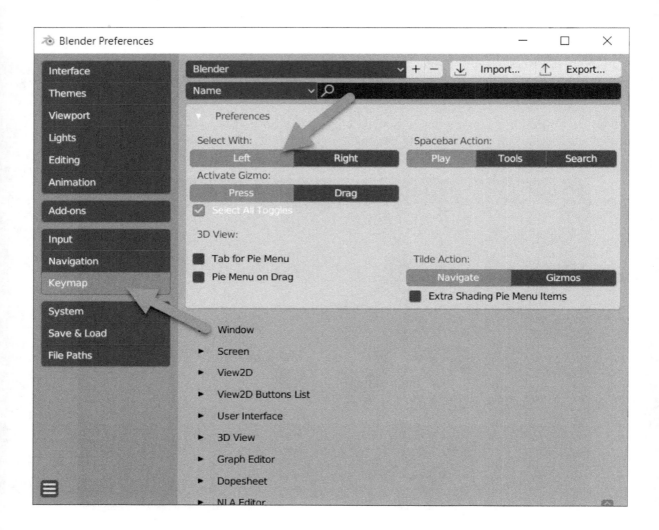

Figure 1.2 - *User preferences*

Why is that so important? Because some additional options regarding the user interface will work based on the selection button, you choose. For instance, if you choose the right-button for selection, we won't have the context menu.

After you set the options with the Quick Setup, you will see the Blender user interface. At first, it may look intimidating for artists coming from other graphical applications, but with some practice, you will start to become familiar with the structure.

In Figure 1.3, you can see the default user interface of Blender.

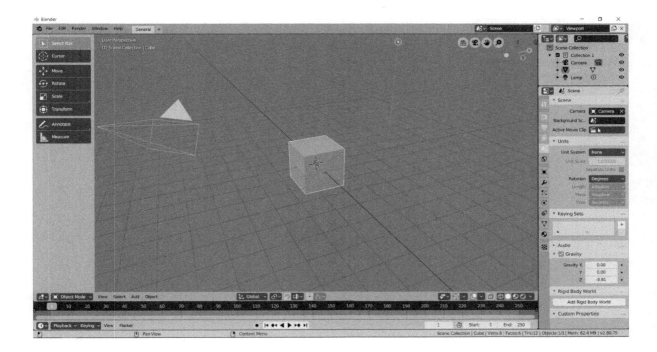

Figure 1.3 - Default user interface

That is the default user interface because you can arrange and modify the editors from the interface in several ways. What is an editor? Each division in the interface is an editor that has the purpose of handling a particular type of data.

For instance, you will find the large space at the center that has a single cube, camera, and light as the 3D Viewport. That is the editor responsible for displaying 3D data and will also allow you to manipulate 3D models. You will work with 3D modeling and all other tasks related to animation and composition.

There are other essential editors like:

– **Properties Editor**: Shows options regarding the selected object to edit and change properties like materials, modifiers, and more.

– **Outliner**: List all objects in a scene and also give access to collections of objects. You can also rename and control the visualization of objects.

– **Timeline**: Give you a quick way to control animation data with an option to add and set frames and keyframes.

In each editor, you will find a selector that lists all other types of editors. If you click at the selector, you can use the same area of an existing editor to get another one (Figure 1.4).

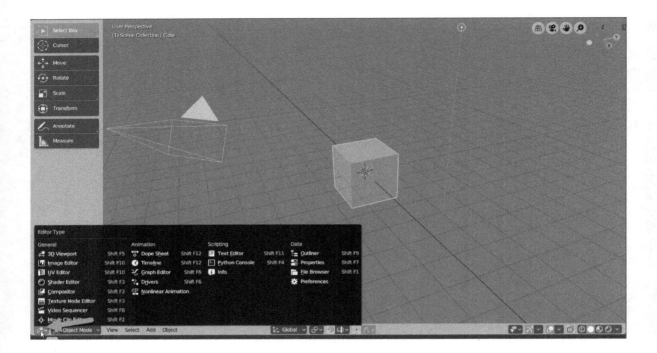

Figure 1.4 - *Editor selector*

That is useful when you want to quickly access tools available at a particular editor in Blender without the need to create new interface divisions.

1.1.1 Splitting and managing editors

As a way to customize the user interface for your needs, you can resize and modify the divisions for each editor. To resize an editor, you have to place your mouse cursor at the border of an editor. Once the cursor turns to a double head arrow, you can click and drag to resize (Figure 1.5).

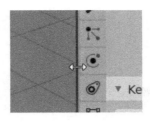

Figure 1.5 - Double arrow head

If you want to make divisions or join two editors, you will have to left-click at the border of an existing editor. Once you left-click, you will see the Area Options menu (Figure 1.6).

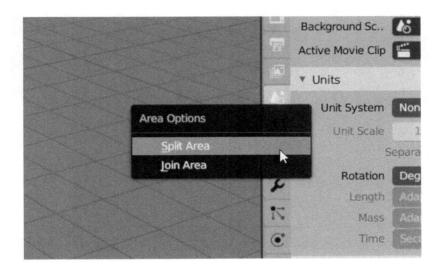

Figure 1.6 - Area Options

There you will find:

- **Split Area**: You will be able to add a new division to the user interface.

- **Join Area**: Join two editors that share the same border.

The new division will always be in the opposite direction of the border orientation you clicked. For instance, if you click at a vertical border, the new division will be horizontal.

To join two editors in the interface, they must share the same border. Both borders must have the same size. Once you start the joining process, a large arrow will appear, which will allow you to choose which area will expand (Figure 1.7).

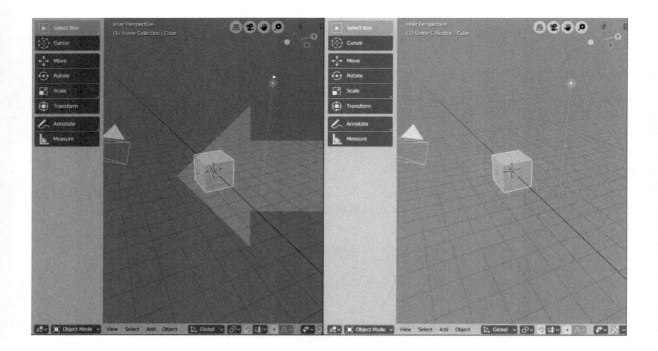

Figure 1.7 - Expansion arrow

The manipulation of the editors and divisions in the user interface is essential to keep you productive in Blender.

*Tip: You can also use the **View → Area → Duplicate Area into New Window** to detach an editor from the interface. That is useful to move an editors to multiple monitors.*

1.1.2 Using WorkSpaces

At some point in your work using Blender, you will have a user interface arrangement that will help you in a workflow. And you would love to reuse that interface in future projects. In Blender, we have a tool called WorkSpace that is a set of predefined user interface divisions you can activate at any time.

There are several pre-made WorkSpaces available in Blender that you can choose using the selector at the top of your 3D Viewport (Figure 1.8).

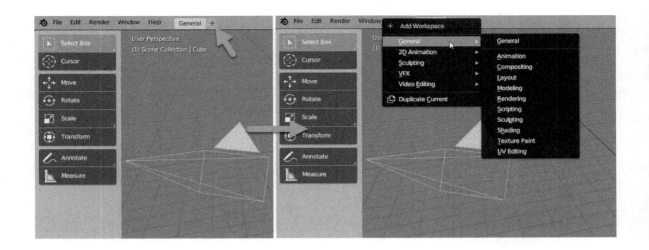

Figure 1.8 - *WorkSpace selector*

You will find WorkSpaces optimized for tasks like modeling, animation, and Video Editing. The Work-Spaces are only an interface arrangement and won't have any effect on 3D data.

How to save an existing interface as a new WorkSpace? You can easily keep an existing arrangement as a new WorkSpace by clicking at the "+" icon at the top of your 3D Viewport and choosing "Duplicate Current." That will create a new tab at the top of your interface. You can double-click the tab to assign a unique name to that WorkSpace (Figure 1.9).

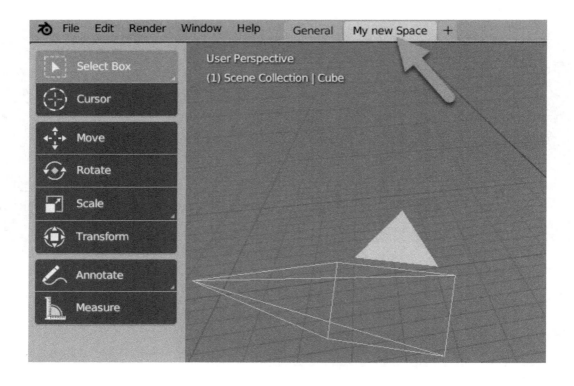

Figure 1.9 - *New WorkSpace*

To remove a WorkSpace from your user interface, you can left-click at the WorkSpace name and choose the "Delete" option.

Tip: You can also rearrange the WorkSpace order at the top of your 3D Viewport by clicking and dragging the tabs.

1.2 Saving files and reusing content

After a few minutes or hours working on a project using Blender, you will most likely want to save your progress. To save a file in Blender, you will use the **File → Save As...** menu where you will be able to pick a folder to keep your project. The file format Blender uses has an extension of ".blend" and will be your container for all information regarding your project.

In some cases, you will also see additional files in your folder with extensions like ".blend1", which are backup copies from your projects that Blender automatically creates.

One of the benefits of saving your projects in Blender is the possibility of reuse some of your content. From 3D models to WorkSpaces, you can get almost all data from a Blender file to later projects.

For instance, if you made a useful WorkSpace that you want to repeat in a new project. You can quickly get that WorkSpace using the Append or Link options from the File menu (Figure 1.10).

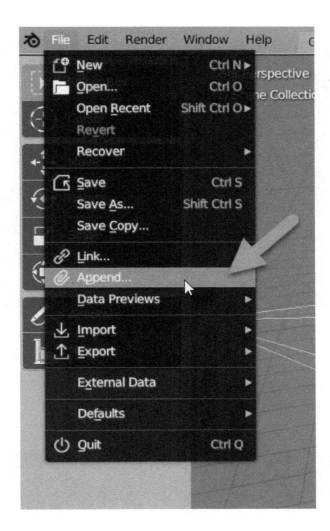

Figure 1.10 - *Append and Link*

With the Append option, you will incorporate the data to the new file. Using the Link option will create a relative connection to the original project you saved. It means the data won't stay at your current project, but in the original file, you created.

If you want to make changes to the data, like a material or 3D model, you should pick the Append option. For the cases where you don't need to make changes, you can use the Link.

For instance, if you want to get a WorkSpace from another file, you saved to your hard drive, go to the **File → Append** menu and find that file. Once you click at the filename, you will see a list of folders (Figure 1.11).

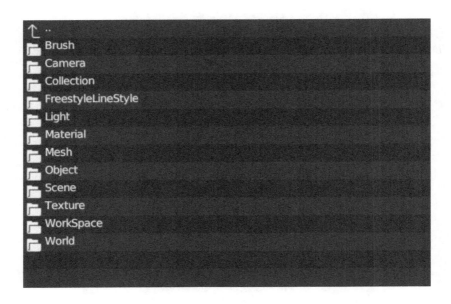

Figure 1.11 - *Folders for Append*

Each folder has a type of data you can pull from the file. One of them has a name of WorkSpace and inside you will a list of all your active WorkSpaces for that file. Select the WorkSpace you want and press the "Append from Library" button (Figure 1.12).

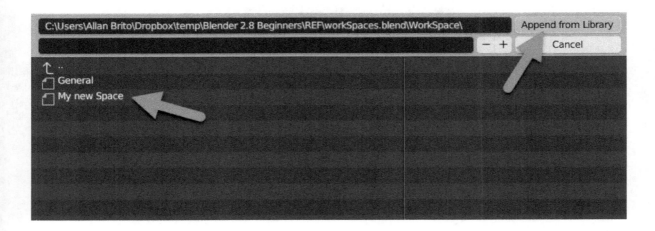

Figure 1.12 - *WorkSpaces in folder*

Once you get the data, you will see the WorkSpace in your user interface. The same process applies to all other data you want to bring from external files. You can use the Append option to pull 3D models, materials, textures, animation, and anything else you wish to reuse.

Info: As you might see from the example of the Append tool, it is imperative to assign meaningful names inside Blender. Whenever you have an object that you want to use later in future projects, it will make the process a lot easier to locate an important asset by name.

1.3 Active editor and shortcuts

Before we start to discuss shortcuts and tools for 3D navigation in Blender, you must become familiar with a core concept of the user interface. The active editor is vital to define where you will use a particular shortcut or tool in Blender.

What is the active editor? That is the editor in which you have the mouse cursor located by the time you trigger a shortcut.

That is important because sometimes you will use a particular shortcut for a task, and you want to interact with only the data from an editor. For instance, you might want to erase a keyframe inside an editor called Timeline.

To erase anything in Blender, you can either press the X key or DELETE. Both shortcuts will erase data like 3D models and keyframes. If you have a 3D model selected at the 3D Viewport and also a chosen keyframe in the Timeline, and press the DELETE key. What Blender will erase?

If you have the mouse cursor above the 3D Viewport, you will have the 3D model erased. To erase the keyframe, you must press the key when the Cursor is above your Timeline.

The concept of an active editor is essential for all shortcuts in Blender. With the active editor, you will choose where to apply a keyboard shortcut.

1.4 3D Navigation and zoom controls

The 3D Viewport is the most important editor in the Blender user interface regarding modeling and visualization of your 3D data. In this editor, we will also have to use several tools and shortcuts to navigate in 3D successfully. To navigate in 3D, you will use a combination of mouse and keyboard shortcuts.

Here is a list with the most common shortcuts for 3D Navigation:

- **Middle mouse button**: Press the button and move the mouse to start rotating your view.
- **SHIFT+ Middle mouse button**: Press the keys and drag your mouse to move your screen (Pan).
- **CTRL+Middle mouse button**: Press both keys and move your mouse up and down for zoom in and out.

- **Numpad 5**: Swap between orthographic and perspective projections.

- **Numpad 1**: Front view

- **Numpad 3**: Right view

- **Numpad 7**: Top view

- **Home key**: Zoom all objects in your scene

If you press the CTRL key alongside each one of the Numpad 1, 3, and 7, you will get the opposite view. For instance, you will get the Left View pressing the CTRL+Numpad 3.

You will use a lot the numeric keyboard to navigate in 3D using Blender. What if you don't have a keyboard with a Numpad? In that case, you can emulate the Numpad functions using the **Edit → Preferences** and going to the Input tab (Figure 1.13).

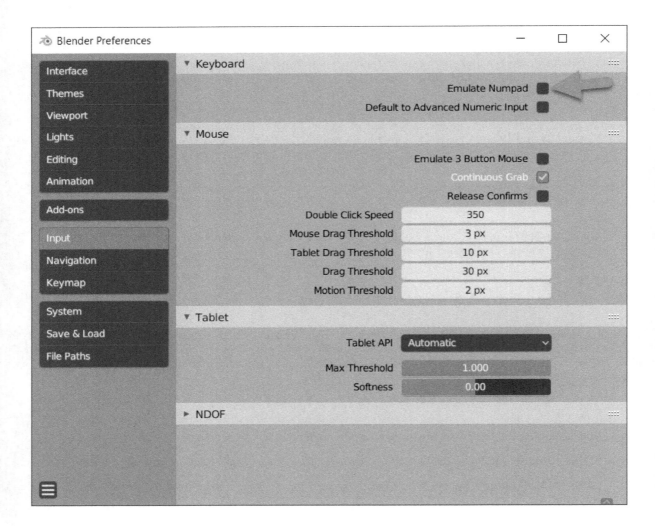

Figure 1.13 - *Emulate Numpad*

There you will find an option to emulate the Numpad. Enable the option, and you will have the alphanumeric keys working with the same shortcuts from the Numpad.

Besides those shortcuts, you also have some navigation buttons on the top right of your 3D Viewport. They will help you use only the mouse to navigate in 3D (Figure 1.14).

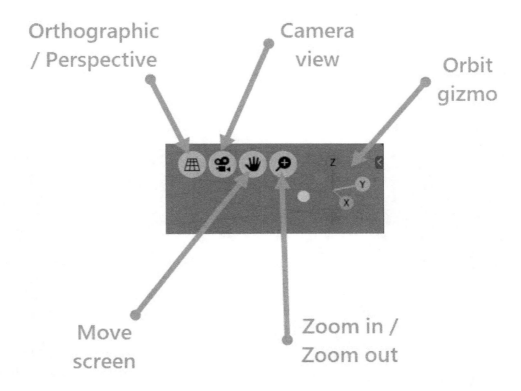

Figure 1.14 - *Navigation buttons*

The navigation buttons have similar options to the shortcuts with the mouse and keyboard. If you want a more interactive way to go around in the 3D space, you can use the Orbit gizmo.

By clicking and dragging with the mouse inside the Gizmo, you will be able to rotate your view. Using the circles inside the Gizmo will also activate orthographic views for your scene. For instance, using the circle with a Z inside will make your view jump to the top.

Info: *All navigation and zoom controls will work on most of the editor in Blender. Unless they don't have compatible data. For instance, you will only be able to use 3D rotation in the Viewport.*

1.5 Object selection

Assuming you choose the left mouse button for selection in the Quick Setup window, you will use the same button for all selections in Blender. No matter if you are in the 3D Viewport or any other editor, your selection options will remain the same.

It is now time to see other selection options to get multiple objects at the same time. For selections of various objects in Blender, you will use the SHIFT key. If you hold the SHIFT key and left-click at multiple objects, you will add them to the selection.

Info: From this point forward, I will assume you choose the left button for selection. Whenever I mention a selection, you will perform it using a left-click.

You will see an orange outline if you keep selecting objects in your 3D Viewport (Figure 1.15).

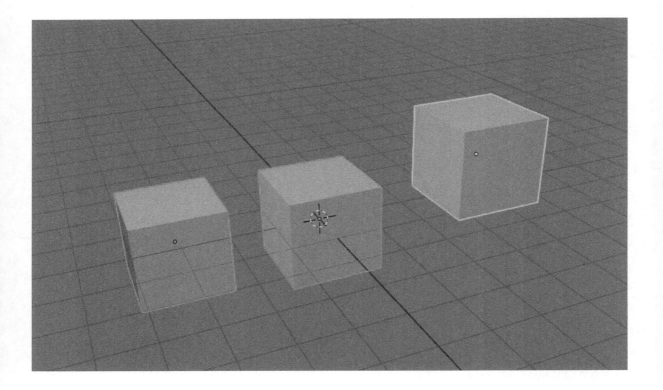

Figure 1.15 - Outline in multiple objects

From that outline, you will also notice that your last selected object will have a brighter color for the outline. In Blender, you have something called an active object. That will be the last object you add to a selection.

When you have multiple objects selected and apply some tools to them, only the active object will suffer the effects. If you have various objects selected and while holding the SHIFT key, you click at any object already selected, you will make this object active.

How to remove an object from a selection? You must hold the SHIFT key and double-click on that same object. The first click will make the object active, and the second will remove it from the selection. If you are trying to remove the active object from selection, one click will be enough.

Here is a summary of your selection shortcuts:

- **SHIFT+Left-Click**: Add objects to the selection

- **SHIFT+Left-Click (with selected objects)**: Turn the object active in the selection

- **SHIFT+Left-Click (In the active object)**: Remove it from the selection

- **SHIFT+Left-Click twice (Any object but the active)**: Remove an object from the selection

As you can see from the list, you will handle most of the selections using the SHIFT+Left-Click. There are also some important shortcuts for object selection:

- **B key**: Makes a box selection, which you will draw a rectangular shape in your interface. All objects in the selection area will become selected. If you hold the SHIFT key while drawing the box, you will remove the objects inside from the selection.

- **A key**: Add all objects to the selection if you don't have anything selected. The same key will also remove all objects from a selection.

- **CTRL+I**: Invert the selection, which is a great way to get multiple objects selected and leave just a few unselected.

Besides the selection shortcuts, you will also find a few options to select objects in the 3D Viewport Toolbar (Figure 1.16).

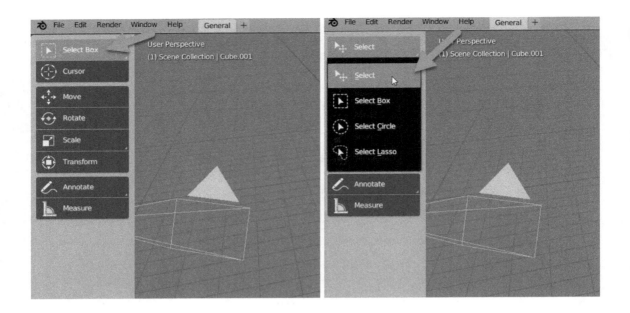

Figure 1.16 - *Toolbar options*

If you click and hold the "Select Box" icon, you will expand the button to display all options related to the selection.

With the select circle, you will be able to "paint" a selection by click and dragging the small circle that will appear on your screen. The lasso will enable you to draw a shape that will add all objects inside to the selection.

Info: A significant aspect of the selection shortcuts is that you will be able to use them in all editors. The same keys will work regardless of the editor you have at the moment.

1.6 The 3D Cursor

A core element of the Blender user interface is the 3D Cursor, which is that small crosshair icon that you will see in the 3D Viewport. The Cursor has an essential role in the use of Blender (Figure 1.17).

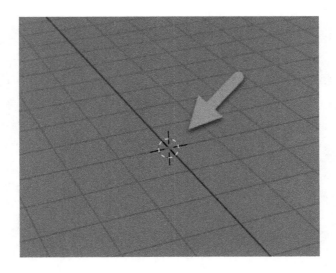

Figure 1.17 - *3D Cursor*

With the 3D Cursor you will be able to:

– Set the location where you will create 3D objects

– Move objects to a certain location

– Work as a temporary pivot point for rotation and scaling

Those are a few of the functions for the 3D Cursor, which you will use a lot for modeling and object manipulation. Since that is a core function of Blender, you must learn how to move and align the Cursor around the 3D Viewport.

1.6.1 Moving the 3D Cursor

The 3D Cursor is important for several different types of tasks related to modeling and manipulation of objects in Blender, and you must know how to move it around the interface. You can easily set the location of your 3D Cursor using the mouse.

You can hold down the SHIFT key and right-click anywhere in your 3D Viewport to set a new location for the 3D Cursor. There is even an option at the 3D Viewport Toolbar that will enable you to left-click without the SHIFT key to set a new location for the 3D Cursor (Figure 1.18).

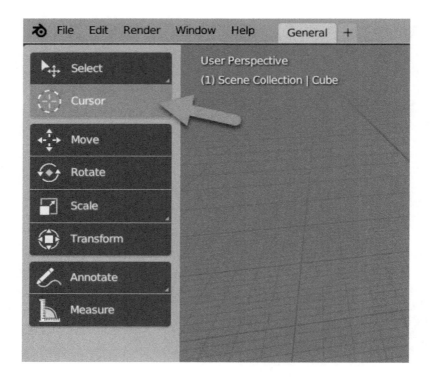

Figure 1.18 - *3D Cursor in the Toolbar*

It is possible to move your 3D Cursor around the screen quickly using the mouse, but in most cases, you will want to have more control over the cursor location.

You can have precise control on the 3D Cursor location using the Sidebar of your 3D Viewport. By pressing the N key, you will open the Sidebar, and at the View tab, you will find the 3D Cursor options (Figure 1.19).

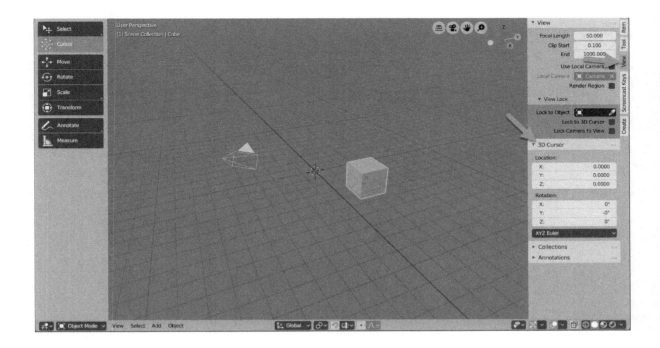

Figure 1.19 - *3D Cursor options*

There you can change the values for both location and rotation of your 3D Cursor. An important short-cut to handle the 3D Cursor is the SHIFT+C, which will center the 3D Cursor in your 3D Viewport and align your view to the Cursor.

The shortcut works like a reset for the 3D Cursor, and you should use it whenever you want to get it back to the origin point of your 3D Viewport.

1.6.2 Using the Snap for the 3D Cursor

By using the selection tools and our 3D Cursor, we can move objects in the 3D Viewport with the Snap options of Blender. What is the Snap? That is a collection of tools that will allow you to align and move certain objects using a set of rules.

For instance, you can get a selected object to move to the same location as your 3D Cursor. You can also align the Cursor with an object.

To use your Snap options in Blender, you will use either the **Object → Snap** menu or the SHIFT+S keys. When you press the keys, you will see all the Snap options (Figure 1.20).

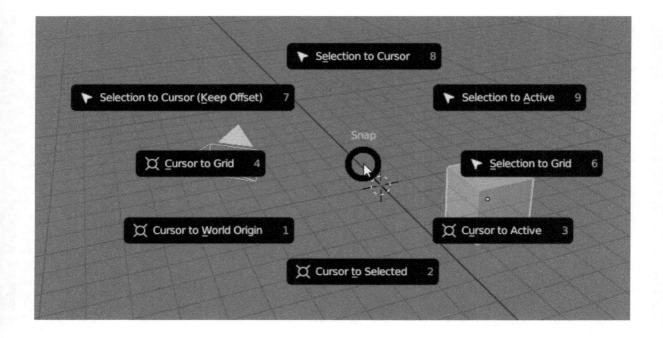

Figure 1.20 - *Snap options*

At the Snap, you will find the following options:

- **Selection to Cursor**: Move the selected object to the 3D Cursor location.
- **Selection to Active**: Move the selected object to the same position as your active object.
- **Selection to Grid**: Align the selected object to the grid lines at the base of your 3D Viewport.
- **Cursor to Active**: Align the 3D Cursor to the Active object.
- **Cursor to Selected**: Move the 3D Cursor to the same location of your selected object.
- **Cursor to World Origin**: Move the 3D Cursor to the zero coordinate for X, Y, and Z.
- **Cursor to Grid**: Align the 3D Cursor to the grid lines at the base of your 3D Viewport.
- **Selection to Cursor (Keep offset)**: Moves the selected object to the 3D Cursor location, but keep the positions relative to each vertex of your 3D model. We will cover more about vertex manipulation in chapter 3.

How to use the Snap to manipulate objects? You can move any selected objects to the 3D Cursor location using the Snap. For instance, we can take the scene shown in Figure 1.21.

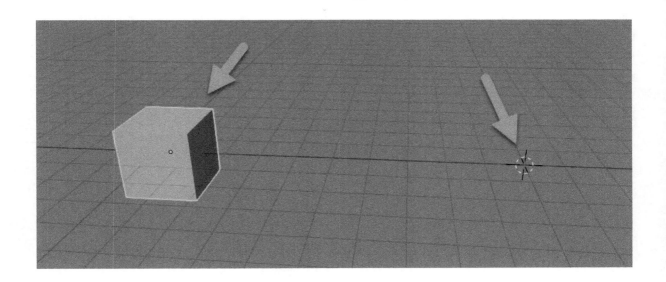

Figure 1.21 - Using the Snap

We have an object at the scene that is far away from the 3D Cursor. If you press the SHIFT+S keys and from the Snap options choose **Selection to Cursor** you will make the object "jump" to the location of your 3D Cursor (Figure 1.22).

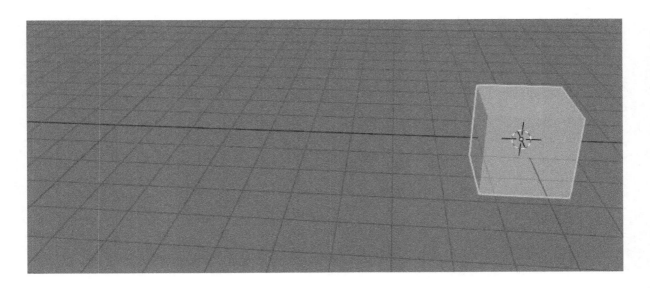

Figure 1.22 - Object aligned to 3D Cursor

You can also choose the **Cursor to Selection** to make your 3D Cursor move to the object location (Figure 1.23).

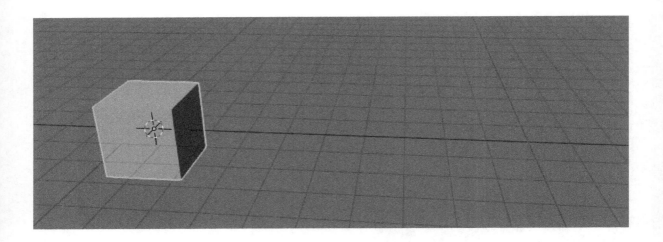

Figure 1.23 - *3D Cursor aligned to the object*

It may look simple now to have a tool dedicated to moving objects in the 3D Viewport. But you will see the importance of the 3D Cursor when we start to work with object creation and modeling in chapters 2 and 3.

Info: The reference point for object locations in Blender have a name of Origin Point. We will learn how to manipulate and control those points in chapter 2.

What is next?

Now that you have a solid understanding of how Blender works, it is time to move forward. The 3D Cursor will still help us along with the book as a pivot point or base for snapping. From all the editors in this chapter, we will focus on two of them in the next chapter:

– 3D Viewport

– Properties Editor

Those are essential editors in Blender and will become even more useful when you start creating objects. We will also learn how to apply transformations to objects like move, rotate, and scale.

In the next chapter, you will start to work with object creation, manipulation, and transformations.

Chapter 2 - Object creation and manipulation

Once you start using Blender and manipulating objects in the 3D Viewport, you will probably want to go further and deal with some basic modeling and transformations. In the following chapter, you will start to use some of the tools Blender has to transform 3D objects.

You will learn how to create objects in the 3D Viewport and also transform them in space. Using the three fundamental transformations, you will be able to reorganize the scene place objects whenever you want. At the end of this chapter, you will feel more comfortable to select and transform objects in Blender.

Here is a list of what you will learn:

- How to create objects in the 3D Viewport

- Duplicate existing objects

- Use transformations like move, rotate, and scale

- Take advantage of the Undo history of Blender

- Start using Edit Mode for object manipulation

- Control object origins with the Snap

- Move objects with precision using the 3D Cursor

- Organize objects into collections

- Rename objects

2.1 Creating objects in Blender

To create objects in Blender, you will have to either use the Add menu that appears at the 3D Viewport header or the SHIFT+A keys. The shortcut will work for object creation when you have the 3D Viewport as the Active editor. If you don't remember how active editors works, you can go back to chapter 1 and reread section 1.3.

When you press the SHIFT+A keys or open the Add menu, you will see a box that has all the creation options for Blender (Figure 2.1).

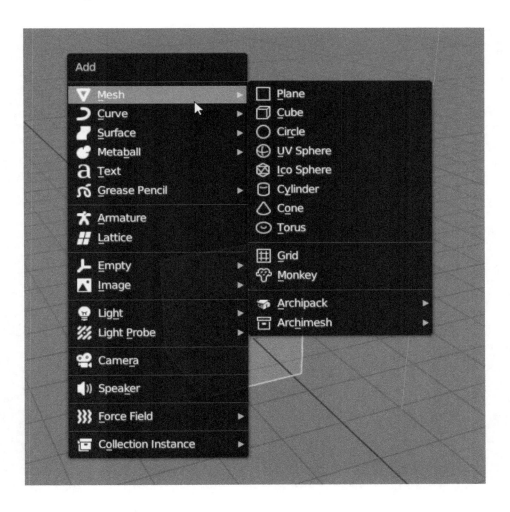

Figure 2.1 - *Object creation box*

You will find options to create all types of objects in that menu starting with polygons under the Mesh group to lights, and also cameras. Depending on your project in Blender, you will need a particular type of object. To get started with 3D modeling, the most straightforward type to manage is a Mesh (Polygons).

At the Mesh group, you will be able to create geometrical primitives such as:

- Cube

- Circle

- UV Sphere (square faces)

- ICO Sphere (triangular facer)

- Cylinder

- Cone

- Torus

We can use those primitives as a starting point for several modeling projects. A Cube can become a chair or a human-head depending on the number of modifications you apply to the object.

To create an object at the 3D Viewport, you must pick a location to create the object by placing the 3D Cursor and press the SHIFT+A keys. For instance, we can add a new Cylinder to the scene (Figure 2.2).

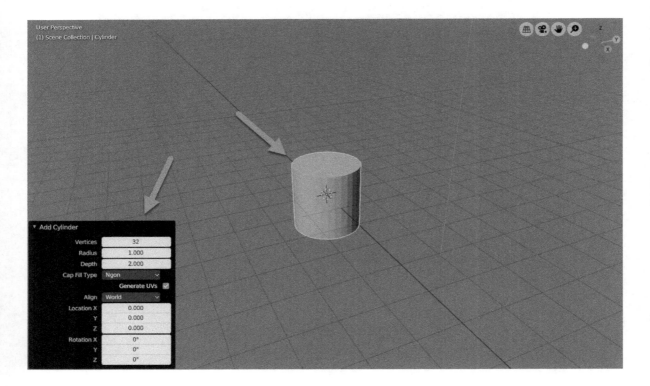

Figure 2.2 - *Cylinder at the scene*

One aspect of the object creation that you will notice is that every time you create an object to the 3D Viewport, a small menu will appear at the lower-left corner of your 3D Viewport. That menu displays some contextual information regarding the created object.

For instance, when you create a Cylinder, you can edit aspects of the object like:

- **Vertices**: The number of sides for the cylinder.

- **Radius**: Distance from the center to the border.

- **Depth**: The height of your cylinder.

If you plan or have to make changes to the object based on that contextual menu, you must do that right after you create the object. Once you create the object and select anything else or perform another operation, you will lose access to that menu.

Tip: If you accidentally close the menu by selection other objects, you can call it back by pressing the F9 key. However, it will only work if you don't perform any other operation. The F9 key calls the "Adjust last operation..." option.

In some cases, you will have to use the menu to make adjustments to the object. For instance, you can create a square from a Circle. You must create a Circle from the Mesh group and change the Vertices option to four (Figure 2.3).

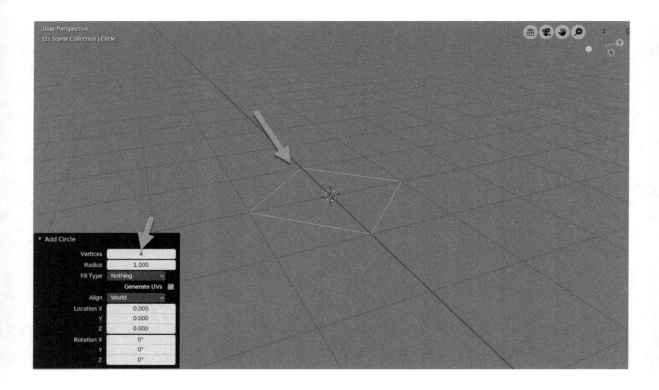

Figure 2.3 - *Square from circle*

That will result in a square, which is similar to the plane option with only the borders.

For each object you create in Blender, it is possible to view and edit some properties straight in the 3D Viewport. You can use the Sidebar by pressing the N key (Figure 2.4).

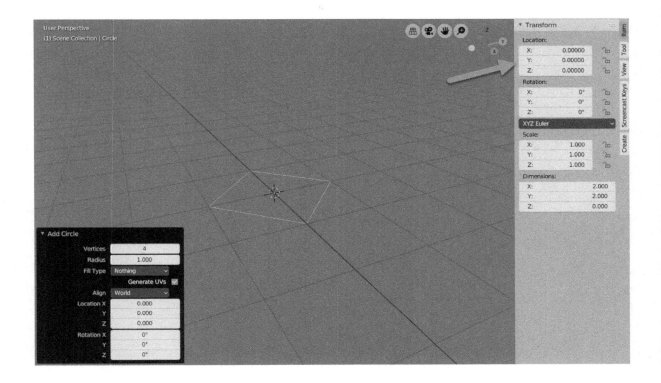

Figure 2.4 - *Sidebar*

By selecting an object, you will be able to change properties like:

– Location

– Rotation

– Scale

Each property has numeric values that can receive modifications in the text fields. For instance, you can rotate an object in the Z-axis 45 degrees by entering that value in the Rotation field identified with the Z letter.

You will also find the same options in the Properties Editor, where you have the Object tab (Figure 2.5).

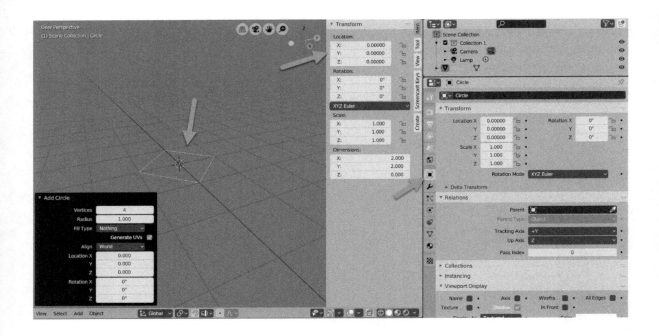

Figure 2.5 - *Properties Editor*

Both options will display information based on the selected objects. The Sidebar has a shorter list of options, whereas with the Properties Editor you will get all options to edit objects spread across multiple tabs.

Tip: *In both options, you get an interesting tool to protect any object from receiving transformations. You can enable the small padlock icon for each transformation to protect them from any unintentional changes.*

2.2 Object transformations

After you start to create objects in Blender, you will probably want to make some transformations in the 3D Viewport. In any software that supports the handling of 3D Data, you will most likely find three main types of transformations:

– Move

– Rotate

– Scale

Those transformations will help you in tasks like modeling and also scene organization. You have multiple options to apply those transformations in Blender. You can use the transform gizmo that appears when you select a transformation from the Toolbar (Figure 2.6).

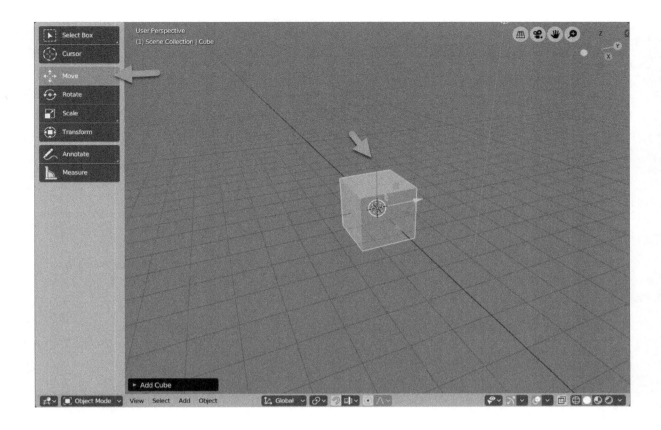

Figure 2.6 - *Transform gizmo*

The gizmo will change based on the transformation tool you choose at the Toolbar. Each transformation gizmo will let you interact with the object in a certain way:

– **Move**: Click and drag the mouse on the arrow corresponding to the axis in which you want to move the object.

– **Rotate**: Click and drag the mouse in the arc representing the axis you want to use for a rotation.

– **Scale**: Click and drag in the small squares at the end of each line representing an axis.

A quick way to change the gizmo type is with the SHIFT+SPACEBAR keys. By pressing those keys in the 3D Viewport, you will open a small menu that has all three transformations. There is also an option with a name of Transform, which will create a "super" gizmo with all three operations appearing at the same time.

Even with the gizmo offering a visual tool to apply transformations, you will find that most artists using Blender prefer to use shortcuts to perform transformations. You can quickly implement a transformation using the following shortcuts:

- **G key**: Move an object
- **R key**: Rotate an object
- **S key**: Scale an object

Once you trigger a transforming using those keys, you will have to click somewhere in the 3D Viewport to finish the operation. At any moment, you can also cancel the transformation by pressing the ESC key.

Tip: *Those keys will work in all editors for transformations. For instance, you can move animation data in the Timeline using the G key.*

As you will realize, after trying to apply a transformation with a key, it will not have a constraint to any axis. Unlike the gizmo where you have to choose the axis in which you want to apply the transformation.

You can constraint the transformation to an axis by pressing the corresponding key representing the axis you wish to use. For instance, you can move an object in the X-axis by pressing the X key after you hit the G key.

Here are some examples of keys that will apply transformations with an axis constraint:

- **G key and Y key**: Move in the Y-axis
- **R key and Z key**: Rotate in the Z-axis
- **S key and X key**: Scale in the X-axis

Notice that you should press the keys in sequence and not at the same time. You can use any combination of those keys to apply a transformation.

Tip: *You can cancel the transformation at any time by pressing the ESC key.*

All the transformation options are also available at the **Object** → **Transformations** menu. There you will find a list with the transformation options.

2.2.1 Duplicating objects

In Blender, you will find that some operations will automatically trigger a transformation. For instance, if you duplicate an object in your 3D Viewport, it will also move the copied object.

How to duplicate an object? To create a duplicate of any object you can use the SHIFT+D keys with an object selected or the **Object** → **Duplicate Objects** menu. For instance, you can choose one or multiple objects and press the keys. By moving the mouse cursor, you will start to see the duplicates. Click anywhere in your 3D Viewport to place your newly created objects.

If you want to create a more ordinated set of copies, you can press a key corresponding to an axis in your keyboard, right after you trigger the duplicate creation. You can create multiple copies of objects in the X-axis using the X key right after you press SHIFT+D (Figure 2.7).

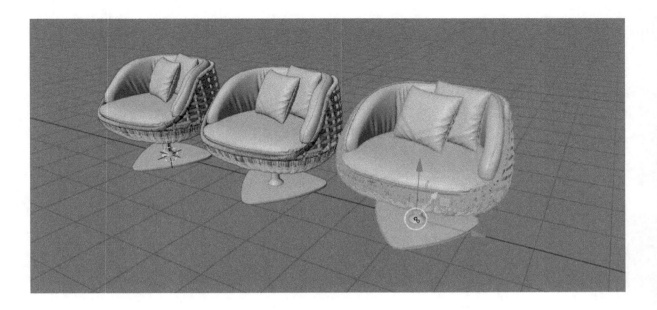

Figure 2.7 - *Copies in the X-axis*

Using the SHIFT+D keys will give you a lot of freedom to create all kinds of copies based on the type of selection you have in Blender. For instance, you can start making multiple copies by a selection of various objects at the same time.

Info: For some operations, you might want to create a copy of an object that is in the same location as your selection. If you press the ESC key after the SHIFT+D, you create the duplicate but cancel the transformation. That will result in your objects staying at the same locations.

2.2.2 Numeric transformations

One option that you can use in Blender to enhance your controls over transformations is the use of values to set distances, rotations, and scale factors. Whenever you trigger a transformation in Blender, you can type values in your keyboard to use it for that transformation.

For instance, you can press the R key to start a rotation and limit it to the Z-axis. Once you move the mouse, you will begin to see the values for that rotation at the status bar of the 3D Viewport (Figure 2.8).

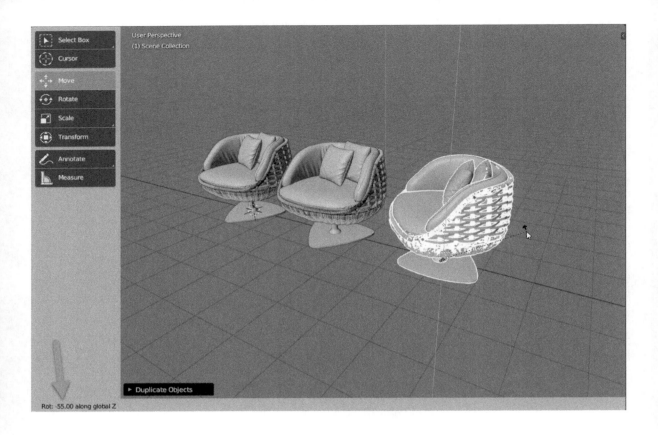

Figure 2.8 - Rotation values

If you type a value like 45 and press RETURN before you click anywhere in your 3D Viewport, you will set the rotation to a value of 45 degrees (Figure 2.9).

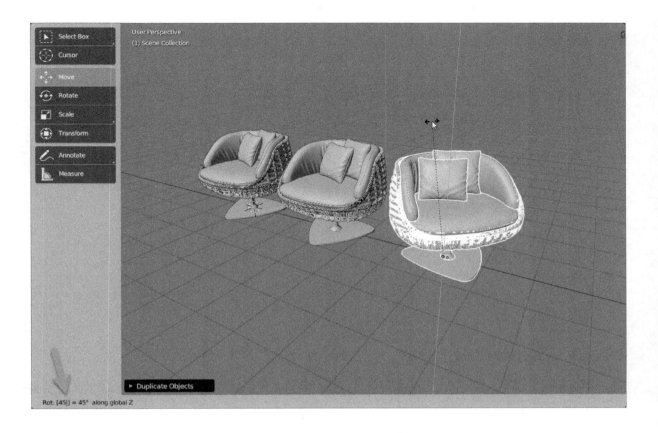

Figure 2.9 - *Rotation with fixed value*

You can verify the rotation value in the Sidebar in the Z-axis value. There you can also make changes to that transformation.

The same applies to a move transformation, where you can:

1. Select an object

2. Press the G key to start a moving transformation

3. Press the X key to constrain it to the X-axis

4. Type 5

5. Press RETURN to finish the transformation

That will move your object five units in the X-axis. You can also use negative values by typing -5 to go in the opposite direction.

With the scale, you have to use a factor to control object sizes. For instance, a factor of 1 will determine 100% of the object size. If you want to increase the size by 50%, you have to use a factor of 1.5 on the scale. To reduce the size by 30%, you would have to use 0.7 as a factor.

The sequence to increase the size in 50% would be:

1. Select an object

2. Press the S key to start a scaling transformation

3. Type 1.5

4. Press RETURN to finish the transformation

Notice how we did not constrain the scale to any axis in the sequence, but you could also press a key corresponding to an axis after the S key.

Tip: You can also use either the Sidebar of your 3D Viewport or the Object tab at the Properties Editor to change those values. But, using them straight with the keyboard after you press a key will be much faster.

2.3 Undoing and Redoing in Blender

What should you do in case you want to undo a transformation in Blender? Or any other tool? Like most softwares, we also have an Undo option in Blender, which you can use with the CTRL+Z keys. There is also an option to use the Undo with the **Edit → Undo** menu.

You will also find in that menu the Redo option, which works using the SHIFT+CTRL+Z keys. In Blender, you also have the option to repeat the last operation using the SHIFT+R keys.

The repeat the last operation can become useful with some modeling tasks. For instance, if you move an object six units in the X-axis but you think it could go a little further in the X-axis you can press the SHIFT+R keys. By pressing this shortcut, you will get the same operation repeated.

Instead of applying a single move transformation, you can press SHIFT+R multiple times to repeat the operation.

Another essential option regarding undo and redo is the editing history that Blender keeps for each file you are working at the moment. You can access that history at any moment using the **Edit → Undo History** menu. By choosing that option, you will see a list with all actions from that file (Figure 2.10).

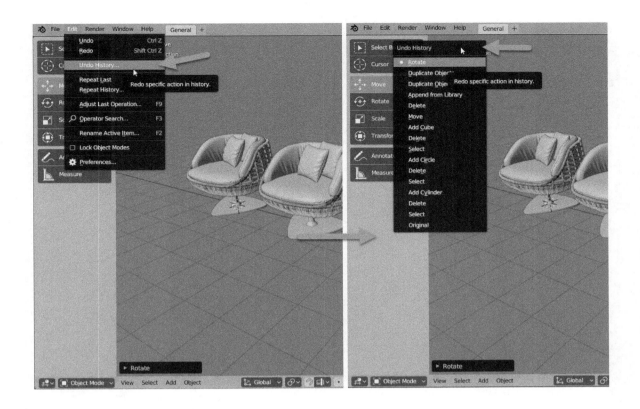

Figure 2.10 - *Undo history*

If you click at any of those actions, you will jump back to that state of your project. In addition to that option, you can also control the number of steps Blender keeps in the Undo History. Open the **Edit** → **Preferences** menu and go to the System tab (Figure 2.11).

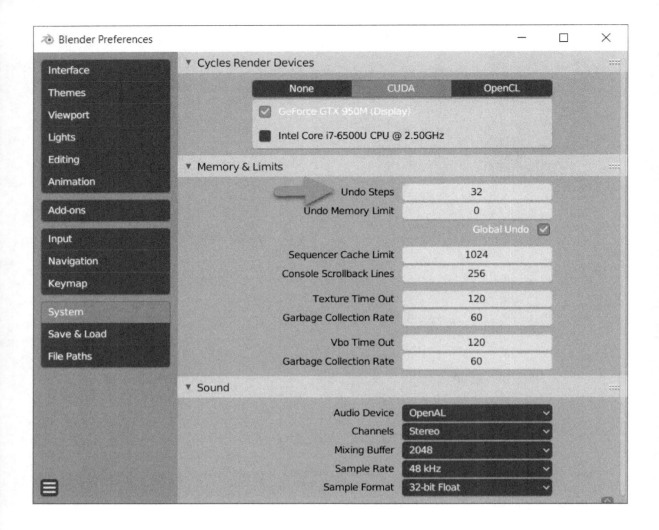

Figure 2.11 - System options

There you will find an option called Undo Steps, which will start with 32 as the default value. You can increase that number, but it will make Blender uses more memory from your computer. Unless you have a good reason to increase that value, it is a wise decision to leave it with the default number.

Tip: Even with the option to work with an undo history; you should keep a healthy habit of saving your project as much as possible. That will prevent you from losing data or going back more than your undo history allows.

2.4 Work modes

Most of the objects in Blender will allow you to choose between different work modes. Until this moment you probably used only the mode called Object Mode for general object manipulation. Besides Object Mode we also have several others like Edit Mode, Sculpt Mode, and Texture Paint.

You can easily see all work modes available for a particular object by using the work mode selection in the 3D Viewport header (Figure 2.12).

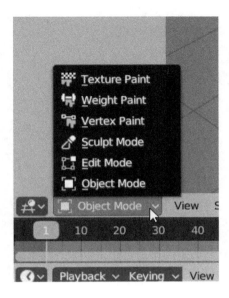

Figure 2.12 - *Work mode selector*

A Mesh object will show several types of work modes that you can choose, and others like a light or camera will only have Object Mode available.

With the work modes, we can have access to unique tools and options regarding an object. For Mesh objects you will have access to Edit Mode, which is the mode where we will perform 3D Modeling in Blender.

Once you select any Mesh object and change the work mode to Edit, you will start to see the structure of polygons. The Toolbar on the left will display options related to that mode, and you will be able to manipulate:

– Vertices

– Edges

– Faces

You can easily change the type of element you wish to edit for the polygon using the buttons located on the right of your work mode selector (Figure 2.13).

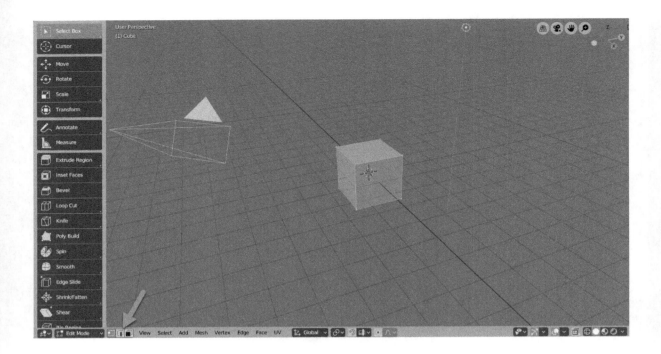

Figure 2.13 - *Mesh element selector*

For instance, you can set the tool to select faces and easily click at any face of a polygon to add it to the selection. You can even mix elements by turning two or three at the same time. To enable multiple elements, you can hold the SHIFT key while clicking at each button (Figure 2.14).

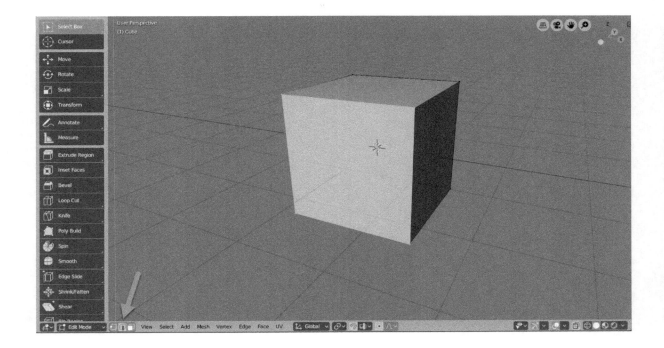

Figure 2.14 - *Mixing elements*

After you select an element for a Mesh object, you can apply any transformation you wish to change the structure of the object. It could be a scale or move transformation, which will help you start working on some basic modeling (Figure 2.15).

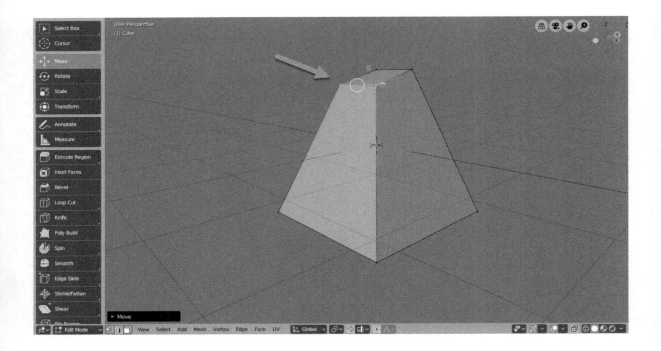

Figure 2.15 - *Object transformation*

The two most used work modes in Blender are the Object and Edit. For that reason, you will find a dedicated shortcut that will let you quickly swap between those two modes. You can press the TAB key with one or more objects selected and it will either go to Object or Edit Modes.

If you are in Object Mode, the key will swap to Edit Mode, and if you are in Edit Mode, the shortcut will make you go back to Object Mode.

Info: *You can use the same shortcuts to select multiple elements. For instance, you can hold the SHIFT key to add multiple elements to the selection.*

2.5 Object origins

Before we start to discuss and work with 3D modeling in Blender, it is important to understand and manipulate critical aspects of objects in the 3D Viewport. The object origin point might help you to place edit objects with improved precision and transformations.

Where are the object origins? You will find that most 3D objects in Blender will show a small dot that has an orange color (Figure 2.16).

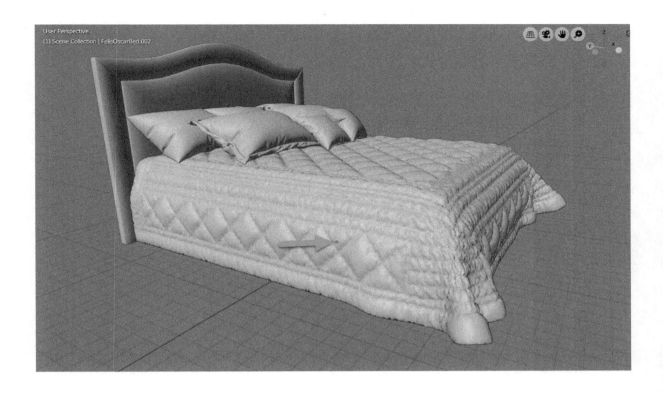

Figure 2.16 - *Object origin*

Every time you set the coordinates of an object using either the Sidebar or the Properties Editor, you will use the origin point location. If you set the coordinates to be zero for all axis, it will be the origin point that will stay at those coordinates.

For instance, when you create a Cube object with the 3D Cursor at the origin of your scene, which is the zero coordinate for all three axes, you will have the cube placed at the exact center of your scene (Figure 2.17).

55

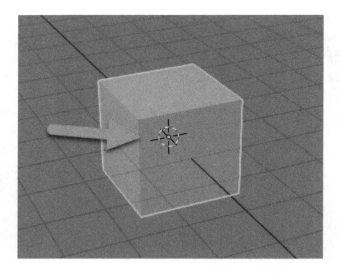

Figure 2.17 - Cube at exact center

Since the origin point for the cube is in the middle of the object, you will have an object that has the bottom half below the ground if you consider that your Z-axis zero level is the ground or floor for your scene (Figure 2.18).

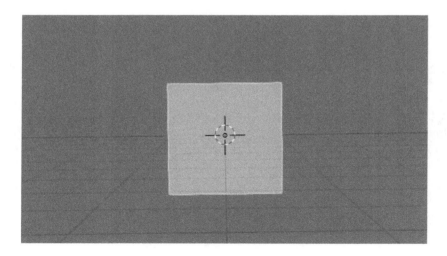

Figure 2.18 - Object at ground level

That won't be helpful in tasks where you have to align and place an object at the ground for modeling. We can easily change and edit the origin point using a combination of our 3D Cursor and the Snap options.

For instance, we can place the origin point at the base of the cube using a simple procedure:

1. Select the cube and go to Edit Mode

2. Change the selection mode to face

3. Select the bottom face of your Cube

4. Press SHIFT+S and choose Cursor to Selected

With that procedure, you will get the 3D Cursor aligned to the bottom face of your Cube (Figure 2.19).

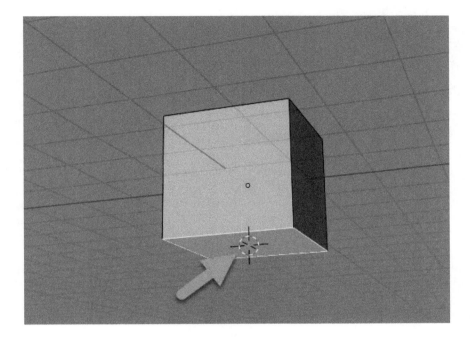

Figure 2.19 - 3D Cursor aligned to the Cube

After you set the 3D Cursor, you can go back to Object Mode and use the **Object → Set Origin** menu. There you will see an option called origin to 3D Cursor. If you choose that option, you will change the location of your origin point to the same location of your 3D Cursor (Figure 2.20).

Figure 2.20 - *Origin point location*

If you try to set the Z coordinate of the cube to zero, it will become aligned to the ground level of your scene.

You can also use this same technique to place objects in the scene. For instance, we easily place the cube that has an origin point at their bottom face on top of another Cube or another object.

You have to make sure the 3D Cursor is at the same location in which you want to align the object. In that case, we have the cube with the origin point at the bottom and another larger Cube that has the 3D Cursor aligned to the top face (Figure 2.21).

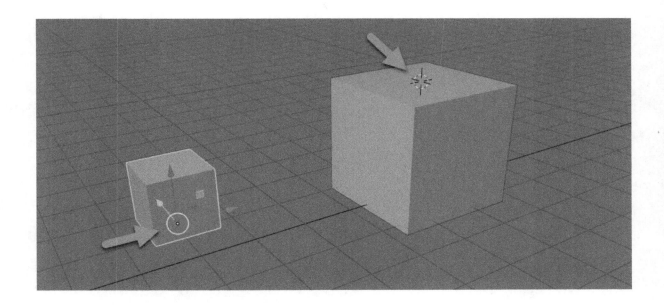

Figure 2.21 - *Cubes for alignment*

Select the cube you want to move and press SHIFT+S and choose Selected to Cursor. That will make the selected cube to align with the 3D Cursor location (Figure 2.22).

Figure 2.22 - Cubes after the Snap

Since the origin point of our cube is at the bottom, it will sit perfectly on top of the other object. You can use the same technique to move and align objects in the scene.

Tip: Always use the Snap to move and align objects with precision controls. The Snap also works in Edit Mode for elements like edges and faces.

2.5.1 Pivot points and transformations

The origin point has another function for object manipulation in Blender, which is to define a pivot point location for transformations like rotation and scaling. It will work as a pivot point when you have a single object selected.

For instance, if you select an object that has the origin point in their center, you will get a rotation happening from that pivot, and all scaling operations will either grow or shrink down using that point as a reference (Figure 2.23).

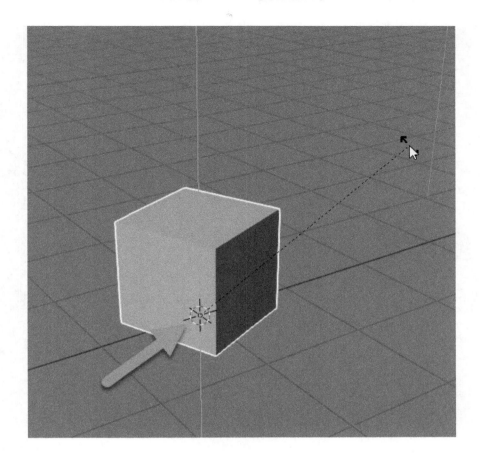

Figure 2.23 - *Pivot example*

That will always happen if you use the default settings for pivot points, which is to use a Median Point. At the 3D Viewport header, you will find the options for the pivot points in Blender (Figure 2.24).

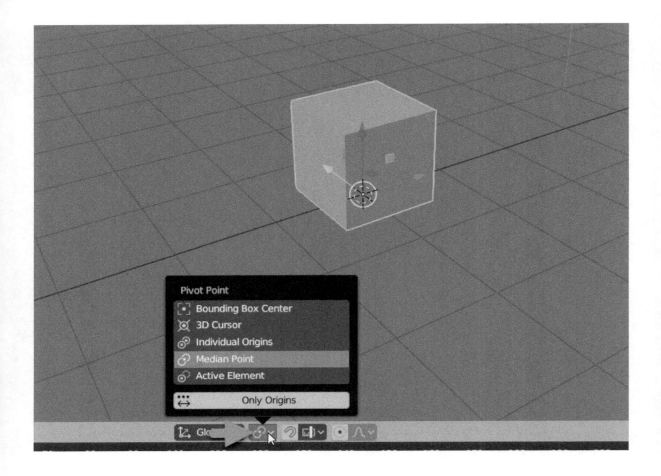

Figure 2.24 - Pivot options

You have several options besides the Median Point:

– **Bounding Box Center**: You will use a cube projection shape based on all objects you have in a selection. The center of that projection will be the pivot point.

– **3D Cursor**: The 3D Cursor location will be your pivot point when you use this option.

– **Individual Origins**: When you have multiple objects selected, you will be able to use each origin point as a pivot. The option is great to apply a rotation or scale to various objects.

– **Median Point**: The default option that uses the origin point for single objects or the central point between multiple selected objects.

– **Active Element**: If you have various objects selected, you can use the origin of the active object as a pivot. The active object is always the last one selected.

The management of pivot points in Blender is an option that can save you a lot of time if used correctly. For instance, if you look at the model shown in Figure 2.25, you will see a wall lamp. The origin point for that model is at the base, which is not ideal for that type of object.

Figure 2.25 - *Wall lamp*

Since the model will align with the wall from the back, you should place the origin point at that location. By keeping the origin point in any other location will have extra editing steps every time you have to either scale or rotate the object.

In a scale transformation, you will get the object contracting or expanding using the origin as a reference (Figure 2.26).

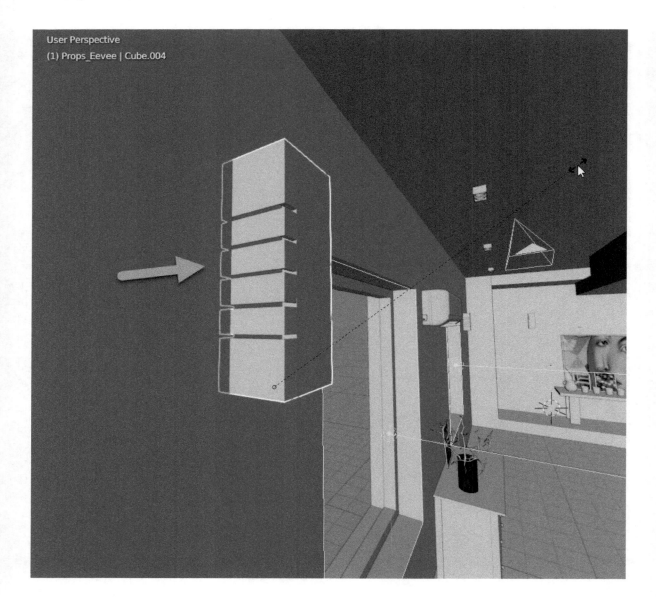

Figure 2.26 - *Scale example*

After a scale, you will have to move the object to align it with the wall since the scale will change the size for the back face. To avoid that extra editing step, you should place the origin located at the back face. It will make the model scale up and down and keep the back face at the same location (Figure 2.27).

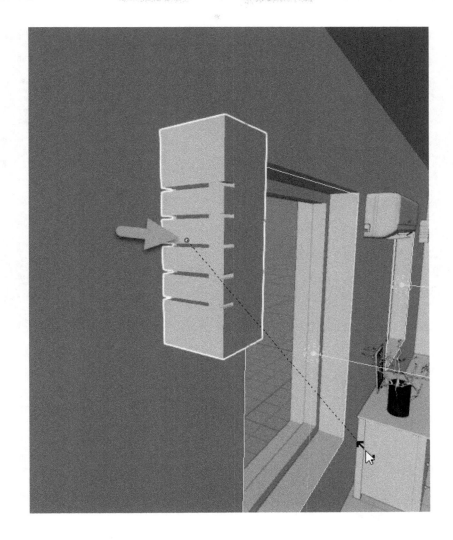

Figure 2.27 - Scale using the backface

You can either move the origin point to that location or set the 3D Cursor there and change the pivot settings to use that location. However, you should try to set the origin point of objects whenever find them to be more useful.

For an object that must stay above a surface, the best location will always be the contact point between the object and the surface. For instance, look at the model shown in Figure 2.28.

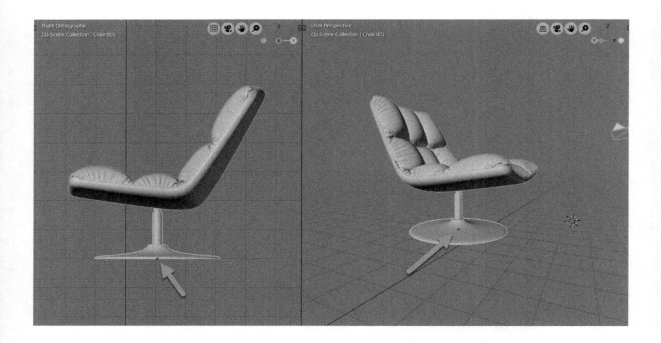

Figure 2.28 - Chair model

The chair model has the origin point at the bottom because it is the most probably place you will use to align it with the floor.

Tip: The origin point is also the insertion location for objects that you bring from external files using the Append or Link options. If you have plans to reuse a model, it is even more critical to set the origin point.

2.6 Object collections

After you start to create objects in Blender, the 3D Viewport will probably become crowded with lots of 3D Models to manage. In Blender, we can work with a tool called Collections that will let you create something similar to groups.

The Collections will appear in the Outliner Editor that is in the top right of your default user interface (Figure 2.29).

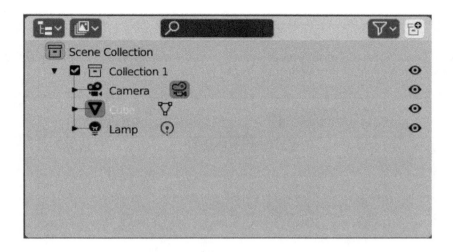

Figure 2.29 - *Outliner Editor*

At the Outliner, you will see the Scene Collection, which is the base for all Blender files. Even if you don't want any Collection, it will appear there as the base for your scene.

You will also have a "Collection 1" that has your default Cube, Camera, and Lamp. All objects you add to the scene will go to the Active Collection. You will see a small circle next to the Collection name showing if it is active (Figure 2.30).

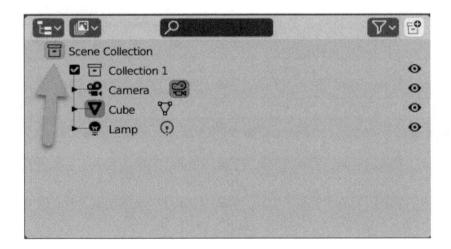

Figure 2.30 - *Active Collection*

To make a Collection active, you have to click on their name. By default, the Scene Collection will always start as active.

Info: *You will also see the active Collection name at the top left corner if your 3D Viewport.*

You can create new collections using several different options. In the Outliner Editor, you can right-click and choose "New" to create an empty Collection (Figure 2.31).

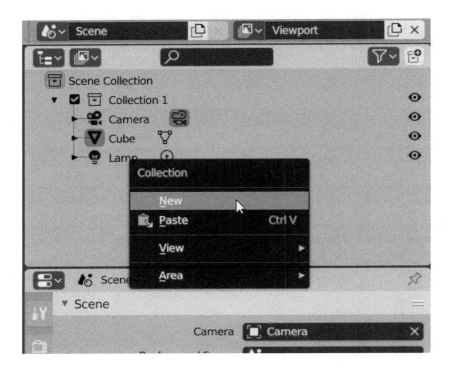

Figure 2.31 - *Empty Collection*

With a double-click on any Collection, you can rename them to something that will help you manage the scene. Still, in the Outliner Editor, you can move objects between Collections with a simple drag and drop. It is even possible to drag and drop full Collections and place them inside other Collections.

Another way to move and manage collections is with a shortcut in the 3D Viewport. If you select one or multiple objects, you can press the M key to open a small menu that will let you move the objects to an existing Collection or create a new one (Figure 2.32).

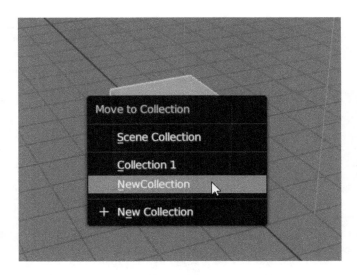

Figure 2.32 - Move to Collection menu

The use of Collections is optional and won't impact your creative results. But, using Collections will give you several benefits:

- You can put all objects from the same type in a single Collection. For instance, all furniture objects from a scene in a Collection called furniture. That way, you can easily select all objects from a Collection using SHIFT+G.

- At the Collections controls, you can easily hide them from the 3D Viewport by clicking on the small eye icon to the right. You can hide individual objects or the entire Collection.

- If you click on the eye icon while holding the CTRL key, you will hide all other Collections but the one you are clicking. Click again to unhide.

- A Collection will appear in the list of objects you can use to bring from external files. Using the Append or Link options from the File menu will allow you to get all the contents of one or multiple Collections.

As you can see from the list, you will have multiple benefits by using Collections in your projects. For that reason, it is important to assign meaningful names to each of the Collections for you to know later what types of objects they keep.

Tip: You can also use collections from the Add menu. If you look at the bottom of the menu, you can create new instances from existing collections pressing the SHIFT+A key.

2.6.1 Renaming objects

As you start to create objects in Blender, you will notice that their names will appear as a combination of object type and a numeric sequence. The default Cube will have a name of "Cube" and by adding another object of the same kind will make Blender use the name "Cube.001".

Each object in Blender must have a unique name that you will see in several locations of your user interface. When you select an object, you will see in the top left corner, the name of your active Collection next to the object name (Figure 2.33).

Figure 2.33 - Object name selected

It is a good practice to assign unique names to each object in your project to avoid having dozens, hundreds, or thousands of objects having primitive names.

To rename an object, you can:

— **Select the object and press F3**: That will call a small menu that will let you pick a new name.

— **Double-click at the object name in the Outliner Editor**: You can rename the object straight from the Collections list.

– **Use the Properties Editor**: Select the object and go to the Object tab. At the top, you will be able to set a new name.

At the Properties Editor, you will have the object name at the top of that tab (Figure 2.34).

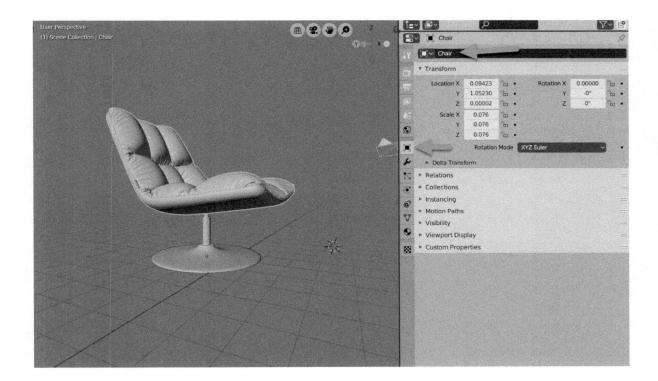

Figure 2.34 - *Properties Editor*

You should always assign names to your models to help you manage large scenes or bring objects from external files.

Tip: If you have objects with multiple parts you can use the numeric suffix and place them all into a collection. Later you will be able to select or instance that Collection.

What is next?

One of the topics we covered in the chapter is the Edit Mode, which will allow you to select and manipulate elements from 3D models. You can choose and change vertices, edges, or faces from Meshes. In the next chapter, we will start to use more tools related to 3D modeling and Edit Mode.

The focus of the next two chapters will be in tools for 3D modeling like modifiers and one of the most used options for modeling, which is the extrude.

With the extrude tool, you can select a primitive like a cube and transform it into several different objects. It is one of the most used and essential options for 3d modeling, and you will learn how it works in Blender in chapter 3.

Chapter 3 - Tools for 3D modeling

The use of some modeling tools in Blender can transform the way you manage and handle objects. Among the options available in Blender, we can quickly point the extrude as the most important and useful tool. With the extrude, we can grab a Mesh object and transform it in many ways.

In this chapter, you will learn how to use an extrude to create new geometry based on existing Mesh objects like a cube or a cylinder. From that object, you will also learn how to cut, merge, and connect elements like vertices.

Here is a list of what you will learn:

– Use a semi-transparent mode to better select 3D models

– Apply extrudes to 3D objects for modeling

– Work with precision extrudes to create new shapes

– Add cuts to models based on loops of edges

– Connect and create new geometry based on vertices, edges, and faces

– Separate and joint models

– Merge elements like vertices to fix 3D models

– Use the mirror mode to invert 3D models

3.1 X-Ray and shading modes for modeling

As you will start to handle 3D objects in Blender for modeling tasks, it will become important to use a tool called X-Ray mode to make your selections easier in those contexts. Why is X-Ray mode important for modeling? The mode will help you to edit certain types of objects that have occluded geometry.

For instance, if you get a simple Cube in your 3D Viewport and try to select the bottom vertices using the B Key, you will notice that only the visible vertices become selected.

To enable X-Ray Mode, you have to use the button located at the 3D Viewport header, on the left of the shading modes (Figure 3.1).

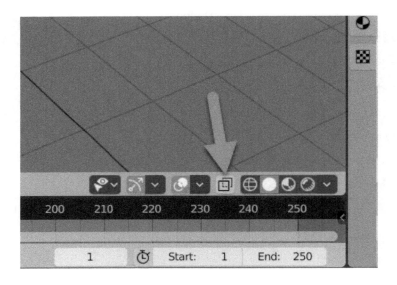

Figure 3.1 - X-Ray Mode

Once you enable X-Ray Mode, you will start to see all faces in 3D models as semi-transparent surfaces. As they become transparent, you will be able to select those elements using tools like the B Key when drawing a box selection (Figure 3.2).

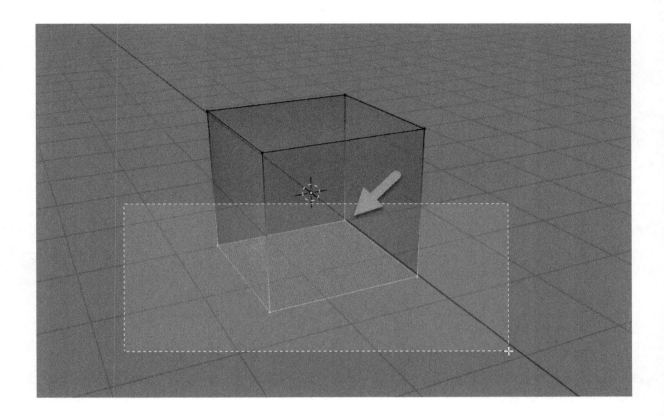

Figure 3.2 - Using a box selection

Using the X-Ray mode will give you the freedom to remain in a shading mode like Solid and still be able to select and interact with elements of your model that are in occlusion behind faces.

3.1.1 Shading modes

If you don't want to use X-Ray to visualize the elements occluded by the faces of your 3D model, you can also work with shading modes. Even being a subject related to rendering, you will have to use those modes to make your modeling tasks easier.

The shading modes are available at the right side of your 3D Viewport header (Figure 3.3). You can also use the Z key to change those modes.

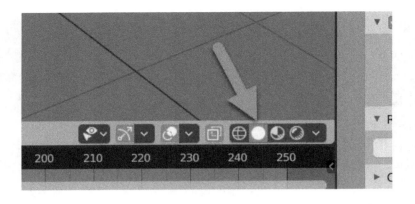

Figure 3.3 - Shading modes

There you can choose from four main shading modes:

- **Wireframe**: A simple mode where you will see the polygon structure of your models using only the lines connecting the vertices.

- **Solid**: The default mode for shading where you view models with a solid color for all faces.

- **LookDev**: Here we have a mode that shows a simplified version of your lights and also display textures for surfaces.

- **Rendered**: The most advanced mode where you will be able to view shadows, textures, and lights.

If you want to work in the Rendered mode for your projects, it is entirely possible, but you might experience some performance issues depending on the complexity of the models (Figure 3.4).

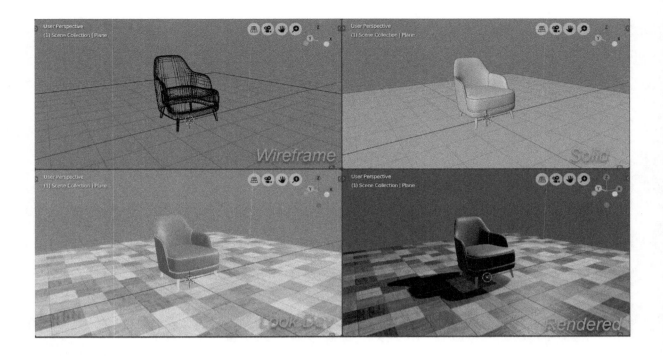

Figure 3.4 - *Shading modes*

For modeling projects, the best approach is to swap between Wireframe and Solid. They will offer the best combination of performance and visualization options for your projects. Even in Wireframe mode, you will still have occluded elements based on the location and viewing angle.

Use the X-Ray mode to make your life easier in modeling tasks to edit and adjust models.

3.2 Extrude for polygon modeling

Having a geometrical primitive like a Cube or Cylinder in a scene could be great for learning purposes, but you will probably want to modify their shapes to build different objects. Regarding object transformation and modeling, you will find that one option in Blender is among the most used tools for polygon modeling.

The extrude is a tool that allows us to select and expand the shape of a Mesh object. You can select either a vertex, edge, or face to start an extrude. With the extrude, you will get a copy of the selected elements that have a connection to the original selection.

It may sound confusing at first, but after using the extrude for a few times, you will see how it can transform any 3D modeling pipeline. For instance, if we select a face from a Cube and apply an extrude, you will see the results shown in Figure 3.5.

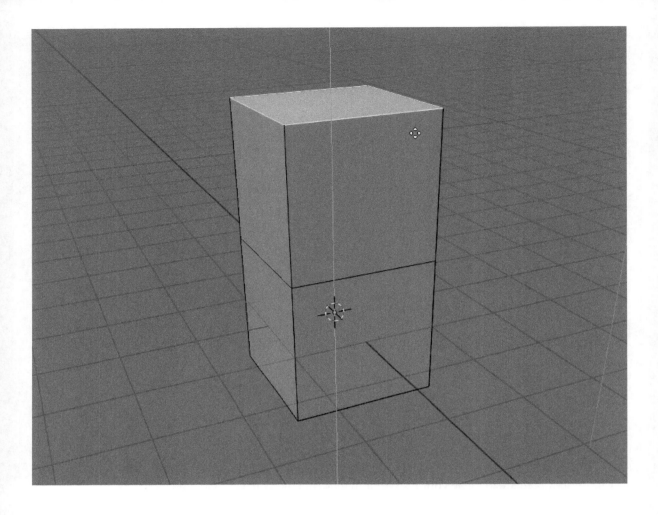

Figure 3.5 - Extrude applied to face

You can also apply an extrude to either a vertex or edge. For a vertex, you will get an edge as a result, and in case you use an edge, it will create a plane (Figure 3.6).

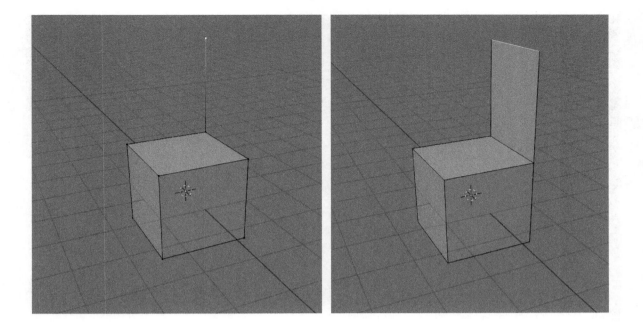

Figure 3.6 - *Extrude in vertices and edges*

How to use the extrude? The easiest way to trigger an extrude is with the E key in Edit Mode. After selecting the elements, you wish to extrude press the E key to start.

If you perform the extrude entirely with the mouse, you will have to left-click somewhere to finalize the transformation. That will give you only visual feedback on the size of your resulting shape.

Like the move transformation we learned in chapter 2, you can also assign numeric values to the extruded length. For instance, if you want to create an extrude of a face that has two units in size:

1. Select the face

2. Press the E key

3. Type 2

4. Press RETURN to confirm

The extrudes from planes will always happen in a perpendicular direction from the selected face (Figure 3.7).

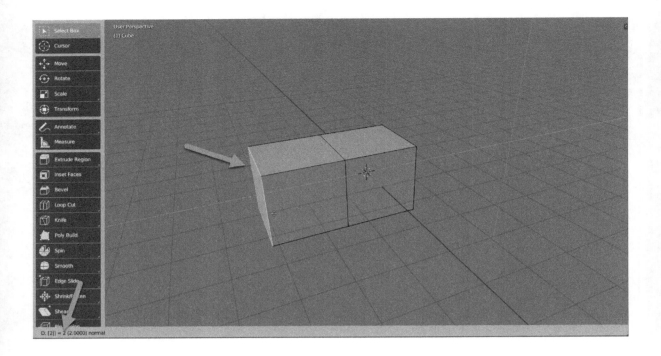

Select Box
Cursor
Move
Rotate
Scale
Transform
Annotate
Measure
Extrude Region
Inset Faces
Bevel
Loop Cut
Knife
Poly Build
Spin
Smooth
Edge Slide
Shrink/Fatten
Shear

D: [2]] = 2 (2.0000) normal

Figure 3.7 - *Extrude with a size of two*

In case, you want to extrude from an edge or vertex; you will also want to constrain the transformation to an axis.

3.2.1 Extrude modes

Besides the E key, you can also trigger the extrude using the options from the Toolbar. There you will find four buttons with different types of extrudes (Figure 3.8).

Figure 3.8 - Extrude in the Toolbar

Here are all the extrude types:

- **Extrude Region**: Select one or multiple elements to extrude them as a single block.

- **Extrude Along Normals**: The extrude will use the element normals to get a direction. Usually, the normals go towards the perpendicular direction from the selected element.

- **Extrude Individual**: You can create here an extrude from multiple elements like you were selecting each one individually. The extrudes will go in a unique direction for each selected element.

- **Extrude to Cursor**: The extrude will go to the mouse cursor location. It will create irregular shapes depending on the cursor position on the screen

Another way to call those different types of extrudes is with the ALT+E key that will bring the Extrude Menu to the screen (Figure 3.9).

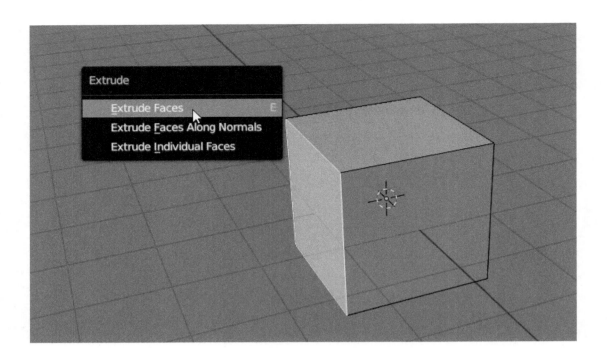

Figure 3.9 - Extrude menu

In some cases, you will also see the contextual menu that always appears when you create objects in the 3D Viewport. At the menu, you can change the values for the offset of your extrude (Figure 3.10).

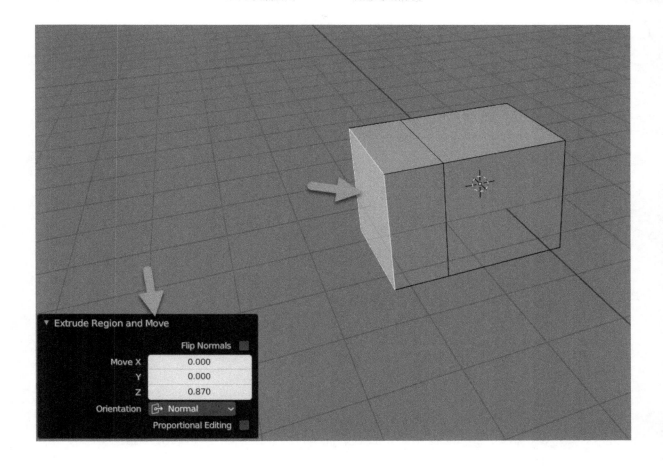

Figure 3.10 - *Contextual menu for extrudes*

Keep in mind that using the contextual menu is only possible right after you finish the extrude. If you start another operation in Blender, you no longer will be able to change settings using that menu.

Tip: The Toolbar options are also available in a floating menu that you can call using the SHIFT+SPACEBAR keys.

3.3 Loop cut

The Loop cut tool is another useful option to alter the shape of an existing object in Blender. Unlike the extrude tool you won't create new geometry with the Loop cut. Instead, you will add new edges to an existing model. The edges will loop around the shape of your models to give you more options in modeling.

To use the Loop cut, you can either use the CTRL+R keys in Edit Mode or the button from the Toolbar (Figure 3.11).

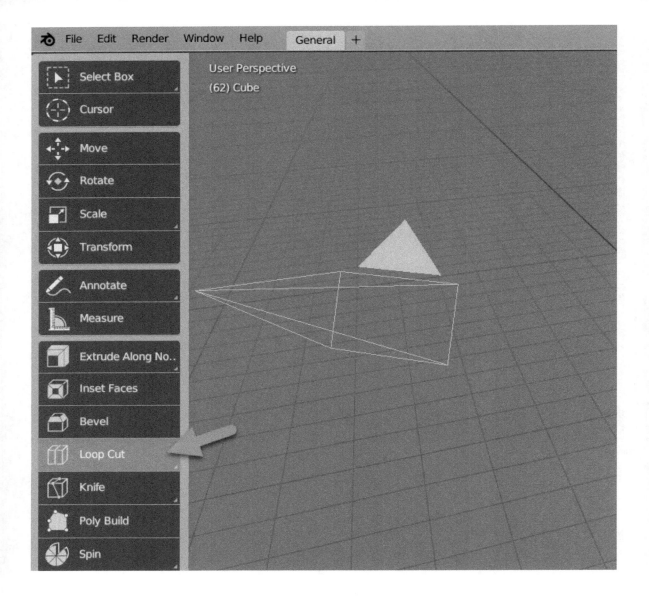

Figure 3.11 - Loop cut button

After you press the shortcut keys or the button you will have to use a small sequence of clicks to create the Loop cut:

1. Move the mouse cursor over an edge. The cut will occur in a perpendicular direction from that edge.

2. Left-click once to confirm the direction of the cut

3. Move the cursor again to choose the location of your edge loop

4. Left-click again to set the location

5. To make your new Loop stay in the middle, you can press the ESC key instead of left-clicking

You can also create multiple cuts with the Loop cut when you are still selecting the direction of your new loops. Before you confirm the direction of your cuts with the first left-click, you can either use the mouse wheel or the plus and minus keys from your Numpad (Figure 3.12).

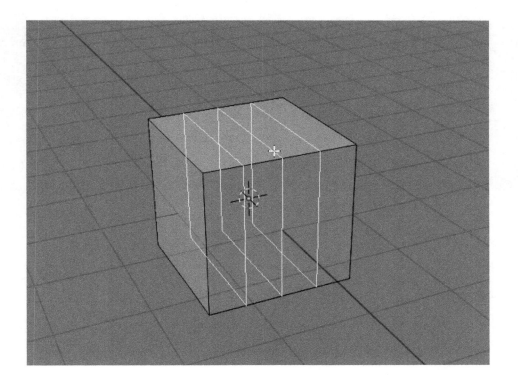

Figure 3.12 - *Multiple cuts*

After you add the cuts to the model, you can select the faces or any other element and apply an extrude. That will give you a lot of freedom regarding 3D modeling.

You can also use the Offset Edge Loop slide to add multiple loops to an object and slide the results with regular distance.

3.4 Creating new edges and faces from vertices

There are some cases in 3D modeling that you will have two separate structures that you wish to connect. In Blender, we can connect objects using the F key when having two vertices or edges selected. The process is simple and only require you to have the elements selected.

In Edit Mode, you can select two vertices in a model and press the F key to connect them with an edge (Figure 3.13).

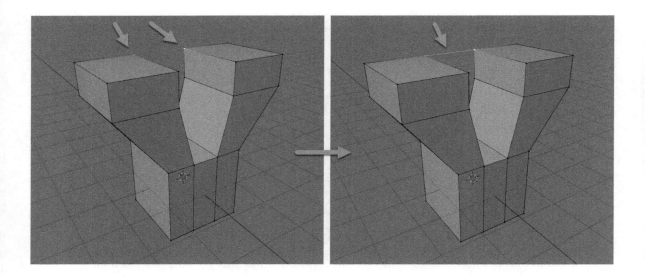

Figure 3.13 - Connecting vertices

You can also connect three and four vertices that will result in a face. For the three vertices option, it is a common practice to avoid such types of faces. A triangular face breaks edge loops and will smoothly deform in animations.

If you have two edges selected, you can also press the F key to connect them with a face (Figure 3.14).

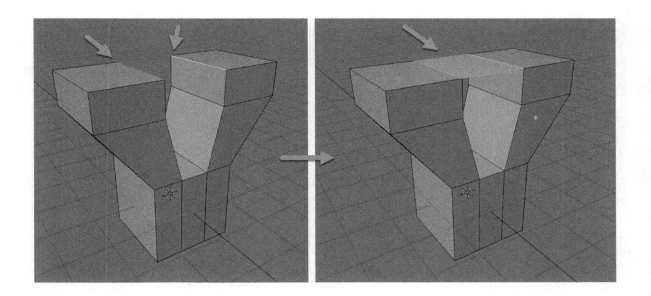

Figure 3.14 - *Connecting two edges*

The F key is a great tool to create new geometry based on connections of elements from a Mesh.

3.4.1 Connecting faces with the Bridge faces

The F key will work to connect the vertices and edges of a model, but it won't help you with connecting faces. To connect faces in a model, we have to use another tool. For faces, we need the Bridge Faces that appears in the Context Menu when you have the selection mode set to faces (Figure 3.15).

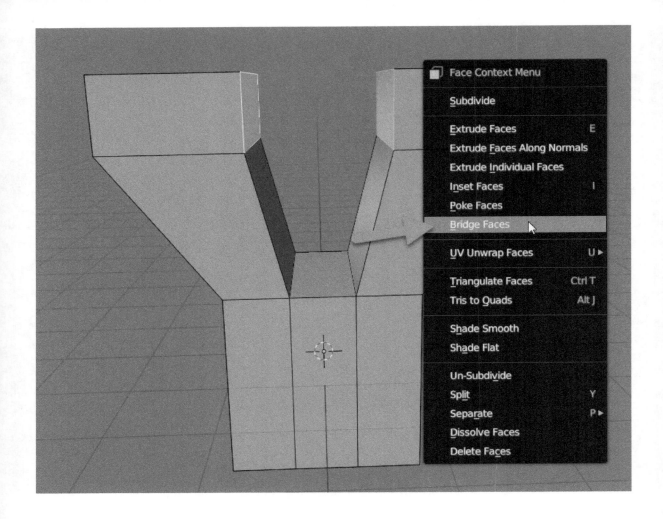

Figure 3.15 - *Context menu*

With the Bridge Faces, you can easily connect two selected faces to create new geometry. You have to select the faces first and press the right mouse button. That will open the Context Menu. Pick the Bridge Faces, and you will get a connection between the two selected faces (Figure 3.16).

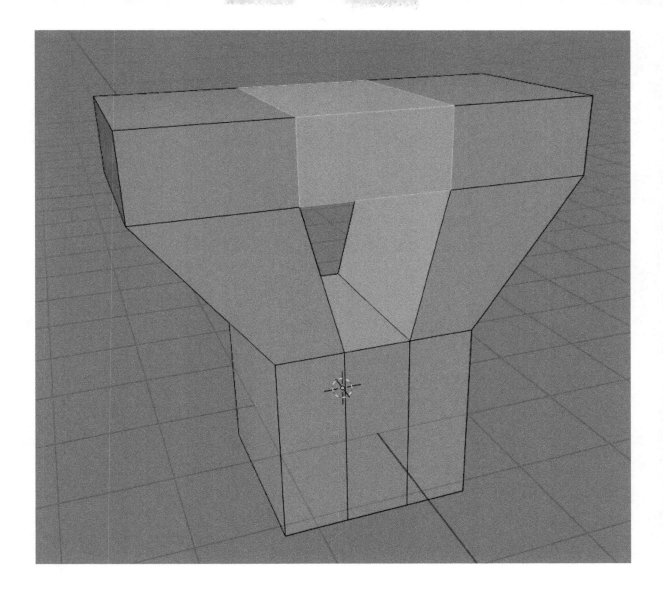

Figure 3.16 - Connected faces

The option will not work if you have more than two faces selected. Regarding the faces, you choose to connect; you should prefer them to be parallel to avoid distorted results in the connected geometry.

3.5 Separating and joining models

In the previous section, we learned hot to connect elements of a model with the F key and also to use Bridge faces from the Context menu. What if we want to separate a model? To separate a model in Blender, we can use the P key with the part you wish to separate selected.

After pressing the P key and choosing "Selected," Blender will create a new object based on the selection you have by the time you press the shortcut (Figure 3.17).

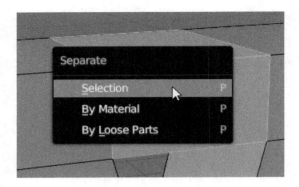

Figure 3.17 - Separate option

The separate option is useful for projects where you have to create derivate models from an existing object, where you want to use parts of that model to start a new one.

For instance, look at the model shown in Figure 3.18.

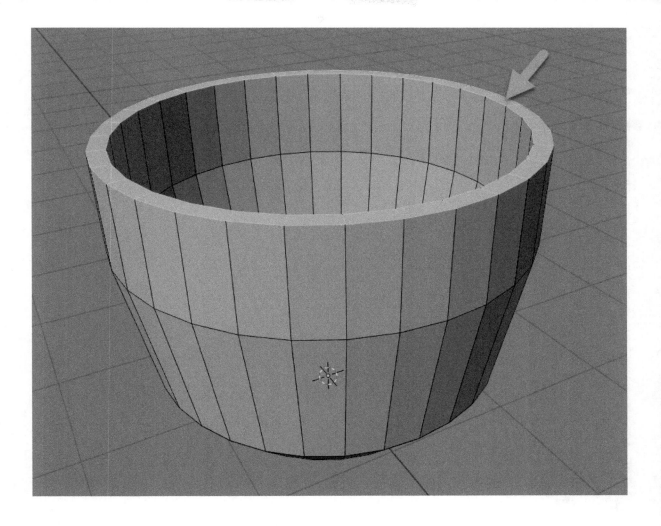

Figure 3.18 - *Model to separate*

The objective of this model is to start a derivate object using the face pointed in Figure 3.18. It already has the correct size and scale for the model. The procedure to start a new model based on that face is:

1. Select the faces

2. Press SHIFT+D to duplicate the faces

3. Press the ESC key to cancel the transformation of your duplicated faces

4. With the duplicated faces still selected, press the P key

5. Choose "Selected"

6. Switch to Object Mode

After you go to Object Mode, a new object based on those faces will be available for you to start modeling (Figure 3.19).

Figure 3.19 - New faces for modeling

Part of the technique consists of canceling the transformation for the duplicated object with the ESC key. That will create the new object in the same location from the initially selected object.

There is also an option in the **Mesh → Separate** menu to call the Separate options without the shortcut key.

The procedure will create an object at the same location from the selected faces. However, in Figure 3.19, the new object is in a higher Z coordinate to facilitate the understanding of the process.

Tip: Later you will also be able to separate objects by Material as it appears in the Separate options.

3.5.1 Joining models

After you separate elements from a 3D model, you might want to turn them into a single object again. The opposite of separating two models is joining two shapes into a unique object. To join two meshes in Blender, we can use the Join option. Select two or more objects and press the CTRL+J keys.

The join is also available in the **Object → Join** menu with multiple objects selected. Unlike the Separate option that required you to be in Edit Mode, you must use the Join option in Object Mode.

You will find that using the Join option is useful when you want to connect parts of two different objects. The F key won't work on two objects, and also the Bridge faces. With the Join tool, you can easily make a new object based on the two shapes, work on connections or other 3D modeling tasks and separate them again later.

3.6 Merging vertices

A typical modeling project in Blender might take you a few hours of work using tools to extrude, connect, and cut models. That will result in your model ready to receive materials and textures for later rendering. In the middle of your workflow, you may have some duplicated vertices that could create visual problems later with modifiers like Subdivision Surface.

Luckily for us, we have a quick way to get rid of those duplicates using an option from the Context Menu called Merge. Using the Merge option, you can get two or more vertices from a model and turn them into a single vertex.

For instance, if you look at Figure 3.20, you will see a model that has two vertices that we could merge.

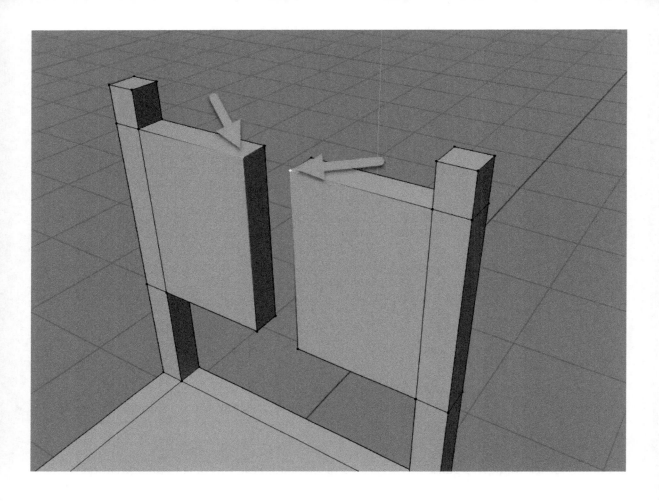

Figure 3.20 - *Vertices for Merge*

To use all options regarding merging, you can use the Context Menu in edit mode. Select the elements and right-click once (Figure 3.21).

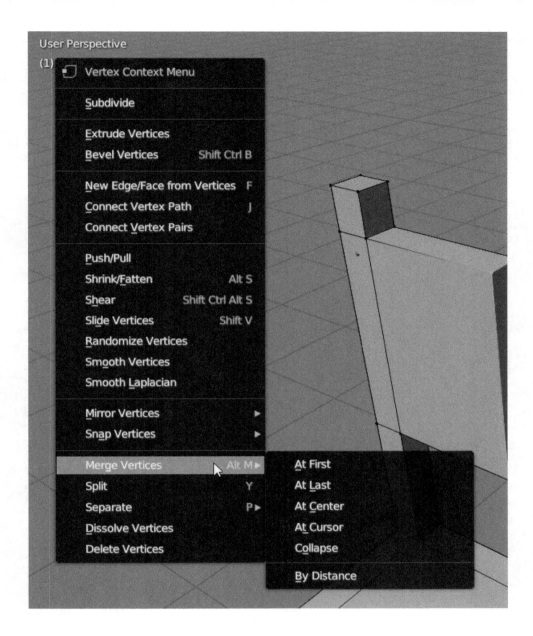

Figure 3.21 - Merge options

In the list, you will see the following options:

- **At First or At Last**: Use the first or last selected vertex.
- **At center**: All vertices will merge using the median distance between all of them.
- **At cursor**: The new vertex created will use the 3D Cursor location.

- **Collapse**: You will get islands of vertices merged based on the distance between them. Each island will merge to a new vertex.

- **By distance**: You will merge vertices based on the distance between them. For instance, using a length of zero will remove all duplicated vertices from a 3D model.

For the vertices from Figure 3.20, we can quickly fix the gap between those two vertices with a Merge based on the median distance. Select both vertices and with a right-click call the Context menu and pick **Merge → At Center** (Figure 3.22).

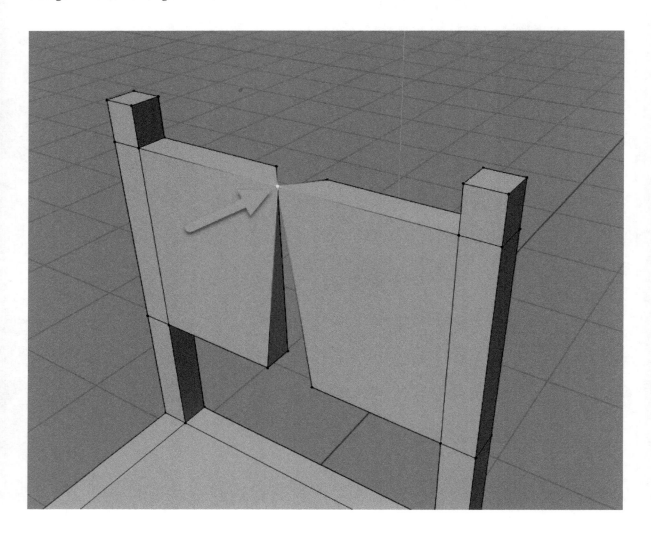

Figure 3.22 - Merge results

If you want to use a dedicated shortcut for the Merge, you can also press ALT+M with vertices selected. That will call a small menu with Merge options only.

Tip: *For the example in Figure 3.22, you can repeat the Merge to connect the other vertices.*

3.6.1 Fixing extrudes with the Merge

One of the uses for the Merge option in Blender is to fix problems created by the extrude, where you might forget to undo an extrude canceled during the transformation stage.

The problem will appear if you press the E key to extrude any element and press the ESC key before you finish the extrude. That will cancel the transformation of the new geometry created by the extrude, but the new vertices will remain in your object.

If you press CTRL+Z right after that operation, you will remove those extra vertices. But, in case you forget to undo the new vertices stay there until you start to see visual problems from modifiers and other operations.

You can easily fix that problem with a Merge using the distance option. Look at Figure 3.23 to see a model that had a canceled extrude for one of their faces.

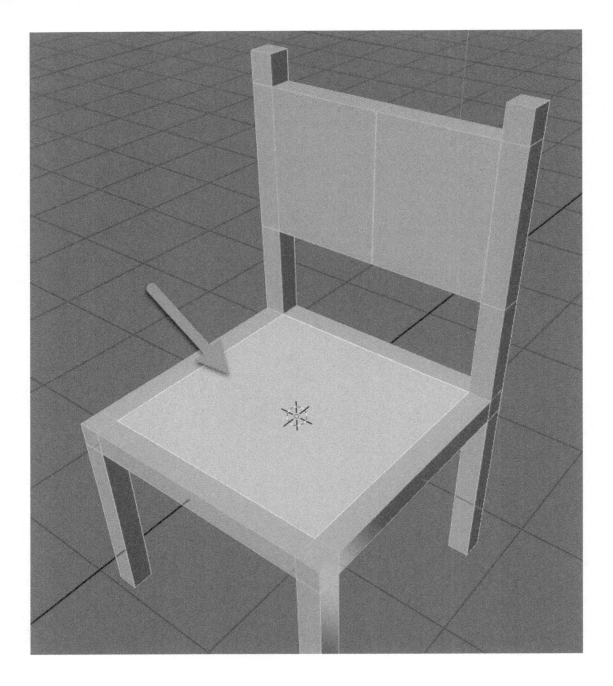

Figure 3.23 - *Model with duplicated vertices*

Visually, the model doesn't seem to have anything wrong with the polygon structure. But, if you select all vertices and press the ALT+M keys and choose "By Distance" you will see a message in the status bar of Blender pointing that it removed 20 vertices (Figure 3.24).

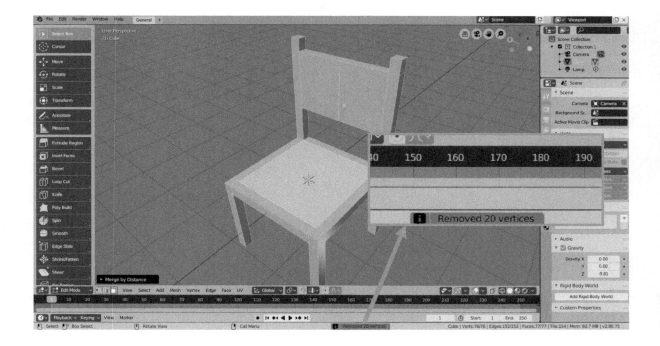

Figure 3.24 - *Removed vertices*

The downside of this procedure is that you will have to trigger the Merge option to remove the duplicates manually.

But, an option from the Sidebar of Blender will allow you to enable an Auto Merge option that will automatically remove any duplicates. Open the Sidebar with the N key and go to the Tools tab (Figure 3.25).

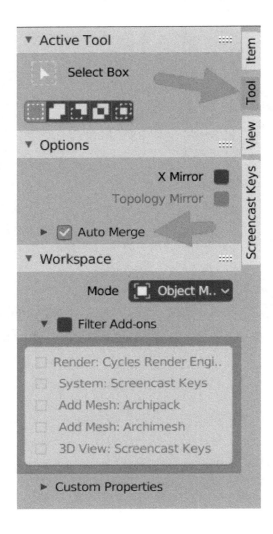

Figure 3.25 - Auto Merge option

By enabling the Auto Merge option, you can set the minimum distance you wish to use for merging vertices. The default distance will make sure you have vertices that are practically at the same location. Leave the option enabled to make Blender remove all those vertices without the need to press ALT+M or the Context Menu.

3.7 Using the Mirror tool for modeling

A large number of objects that are subject of a 3D modeling in Blender will present some kind of symmetry. Working in any object that has a symmetrical side will make your life a lot easier because we can create only half of the shape and later mirror the other side.

In Blender, you will find a few options to work with symmetrical models starting with the Mirror tool and going up until the Mirror Modifier that we will use in Chapter 4.

The Mirror tool in Blender works with the CTRL+M key with an object selected. You won't get a mirrored copy with the tool, but an inverted version of the model. For instance, we can take the model shown in Figure 3.26, that represents only half of a model.

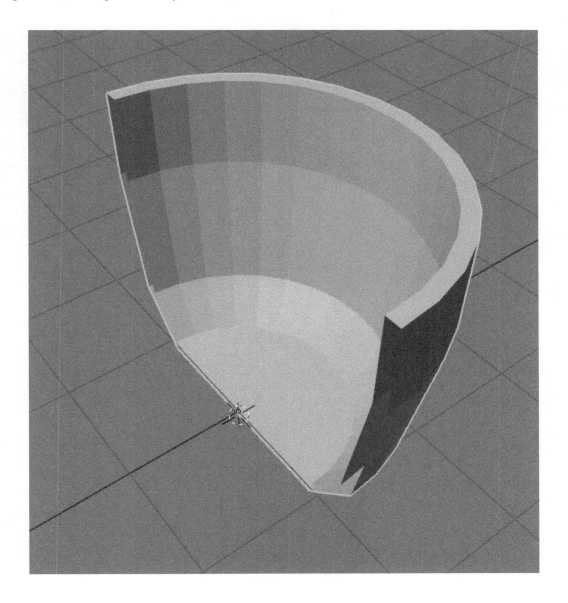

Figure 3.26 - Half of a model

If you go to Object Mode and press CTRL+M or use the **Object** → **Mirror** menu, you can invert the object shape. For the shortcut, you must press a key representing the axis in which the mirror will happen (Figure 3.27).

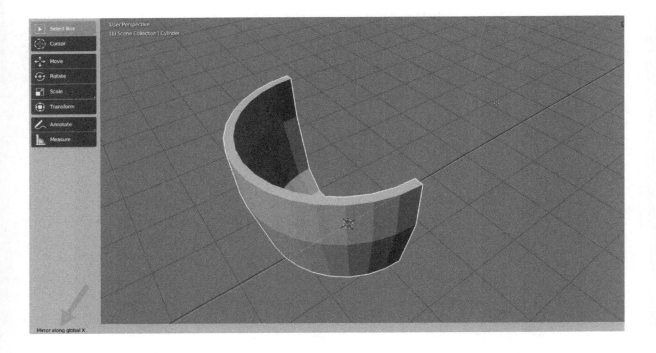

Figure 3.27 - Mirror axis ·

By choosing the **Object** → **Mirror** menu, you can pick the axis you want to use from the list of options. The result will be a flipped version of the model. By using a SHIFT+D before you make the mirror, it will be possible to create an inverted version of the model using a duplicate.

Using a move transformation with the flipped duplicate will make it possible to create the full model with a symmetrical side (Figure 3.28).

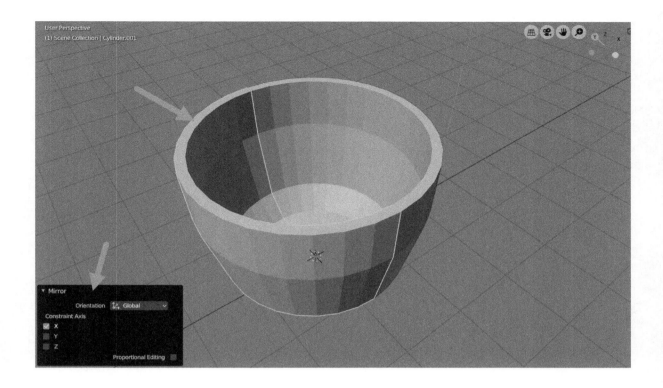

Figure 3.28 - *Full model with both sides*

Since they will be different objects, you can use a CTRL+J to join them and later apply a Merge using the distance option. It will remove all duplicated vertices.

Tip: A trick used by some artists to apply a mirror using the Scale transformation consists in a scale with -100% of the object size. For instance, select the object and press the S key. Type -1 as the factor to get a mirror image of that model.

What is next?

The extrude is an incredible tool and is by far one of the highlights of this chapter, but it won't solve all modeling challenges alone. You will still need additional tools to create complex models.

We will learn in the next chapter how to use some of those tools in the modifiers section, where you will apply smoothing to 3D models and also several replication modes to use patterns for modeling.

Besides modifies, you will also learn how to work with rounded profiles with the Spin tool, which will combine the use of an extrude with a rotation. That will increase the number of options to create 3D models in Blender and give you more freedom to make complex objects.

Chapter 4 - Modeling techniques and resources

With the modeling tools from Blender, we can go much further than just using extrudes to create 3D models. A particular type of object called Modifier will help you with several options to create complex shapes from primitives.

One of the most useful modifiers is the Subdivision Surface, which will allow you to smooth polygons and create organic shapes.

Besides modifiers, we will also learn how to manage tools like the Spin that can create round shapes working like rotation and extrude mix. If you follow the rules on how to use the Spin, you will get unique shapes that wouldn't be possible with the extrude.

Here is a list of what you will learn:

– How to apply and manage modifiers

– Use the Subdivision surface modifier

– Control the smoothness of the Subdivision Surface

– Set the radius for the Subdivision Surface

– Apply different types of shading for models

– Use the Mirror modifier for symmetrical modeling

– Compose unique shapes with the Boolean

– Create models based on patterns with the Array

– Make round shapes with the Spin

– Use the proportional editing tools

4.1 Modifiers for modeling

In Blender, you will find a long list with tools and options regarding modeling that will help you with multiple projects. Some of those options will give you an extra level of flexibility in those tasks because they offer an easy way to enable and disable aspects of your modeling.

With the modifiers, you have a long list of tools that can change the structure of your model in several ways. You will find the modifiers at the Properties Editor in the Modifiers tab (Figure 4.1).

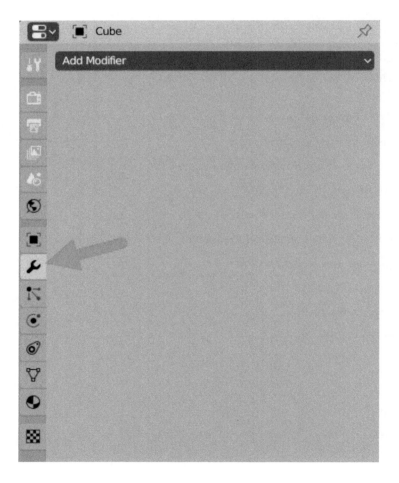

Figure 4.1 - *Modifiers for modeling*

The modifiers will help you in several tasks and not only modeling, but we will start to work with them to transform some of your 3D objects. Each modifier applies to a single object, and that object will suffer the effects of the modifier. Once you add a modifier to an object, it will appear in the Properties Editor at the Modifier tab (Figure 4.2).

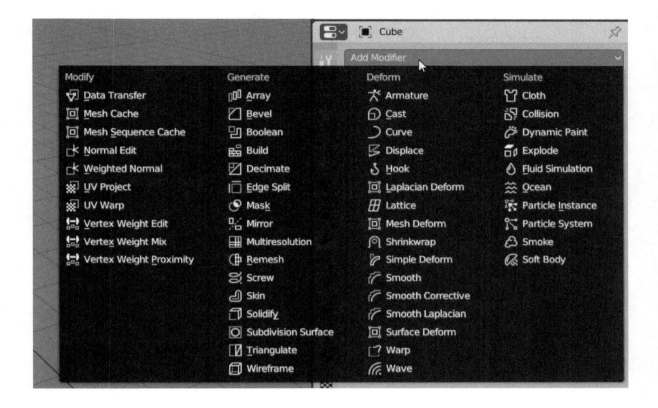

Figure 4.2 - Modifier list

A few aspects of modifiers that you should keep in mind:

– You can add as many modifiers to an object as you wish.

– The modifiers will stack on top of each other at the list.

– Modifiers will transform the model following the order in which they appear in the stack. Starting with the top modifier and following the order until the bottom.

– At any moment, you can reorder or remove a modifier from an object to stop the transformation.

Each modifier will display a few common controls to manage how it appears in the stack and also allow you to copy and also apply the effects of each modifier. In Figure 4.3, you can see a list with the available controls.

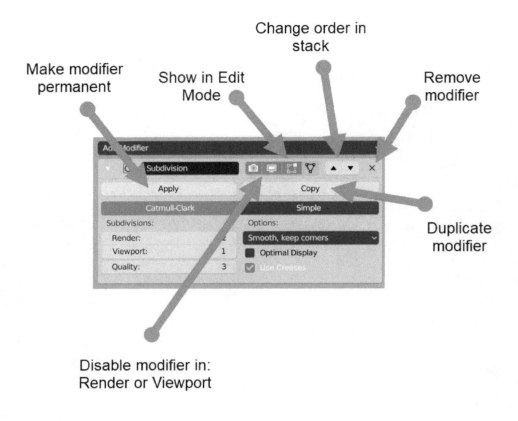

Figure 4.3 - *Modifier controls*

An important aspect of each modifier is that you will lose the effects it produces once you remove the modifier from the object. If you want to make the effects permanent, you should use the "Apply" button available in each modifier. After using that button, the modifier will disappear from the list, and the effects will become part of the object.

That will be useful when you have a project that must use an object resulting from multiple modifiers, which you will also use as a reference to start modeling.

Tip: Before applying the effects of a modifier, you can make a backup copy of your objects and place it to a different collection. Hide that collection for that to serve only as a backup copy.

4.2 Subdivision Surface modifier

One of the most used modifiers that you can use for your projects is the Subdivision Surface, which will smooth your 3D models by adding lots of new faces to the object. The modifier is the primary tool for techniques such as mesh modeling.

Because you can use models with a low polygon count that have a more geometrical shape, and later use the modifier to smooth the object shape. In Figure 4.4, you can see an example of the results of a Subdivision Surface Modifier.

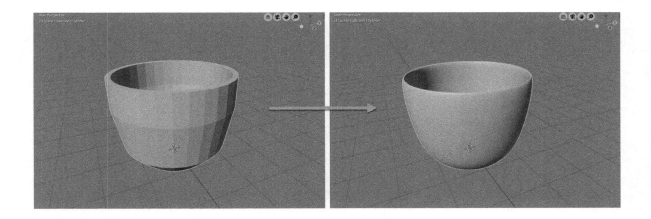

Figure 4.4 - Smoothing 3D model

To use that modifier you will have to select the object you wish to use first and apply the Subdivision Surface from the modifier list. After you apply the modifier, you can adjust the level of smoothness of the object using the settings available at the modifier (Figure 4.5).

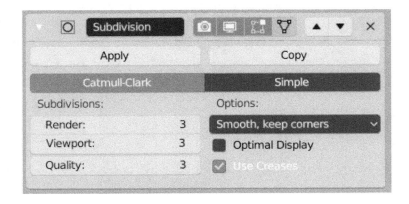

Figure 4.5 - Subdivision settings

What will determine the smoothes of your model is the method you use and also how many subdivisions it applies to the object. At the top you will see two main types of subdivisions:

– **Catmull-Clark**: If you want a full smoothing of your model with rounded shapes, you should use this method.

– **Simple**: For projects where you want only new faces and divisions but no smoothing, you can use the simple option.

The level of subdivisions will allow you to set different values for the 3D Viewport and Render. Usually, you will use a lower value for the 3D Viewport and a higher level for the Render. The reason for that is because a model with a high level of subdivisions may add a significant computational load to your computer.

You will notice that changing the zoom and even swapping between Object and Edit Modes might start to show a lag when you have high-density objects in the 3D Viewport.

A value of two for the 3D Viewport and three for Render will produce great results most of the time. Unless you have a model that requires more subdivisions, you can use two for the viewport and three for render. At Figure 4.6, you can see the difference between using two and three for subdivisions.

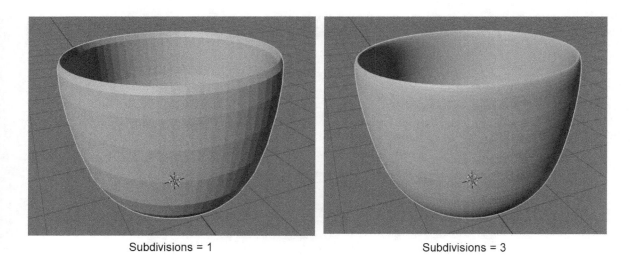

Subdivisions = 1   Subdivisions = 3

Figure 4.6 - *Different levels of subdivision*

With the precision value, you can control the accuracy of how your modifier will place the vertices concerning the original object. Higher values will result in more precision locations but will add more computational load to the model.

4.2.1 Controlling surface smoothing

Even after using the Subdivision Surface modifier in a model, you might still see a few faces showing up at an object shape. The modifier will help you to create a smooth surface for the model, but won't remove visible borders from the faces it creates (Figure 4.7).

Figure 4.7 - *Face borders in objects*

To smooth the surface of any model we have two options in Blender called:

– Shade smooth

– Shade flat

By default, all models you create will use the Shade flat option, and in case you want to remove the visible borders between objects, you will have to apply a Shade smooth. The option is available when you are in Object Mode. With an object selected, you can right-click to open the Context menu (Figure 4.8).

Figure 4.8 - *Context menu*

There you will see the Shading options, and by choosing Shade Smooth, you can remove the visible border between each face (Figure 4.9).

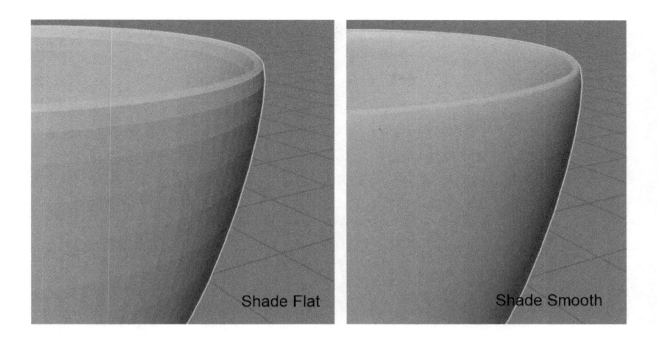

Shade Flat

Shade Smooth

Figure 4.9 - *Results of a Shade Smooth*

The option is also available at the Object Menu when you are in Object Mode. After you apply the Subdivision Surface modifier to any object, you can enable the Shade Smooth to make it have a surface with no visible borders between each face.

4.2.2 Fixing smoothing problems

In the process of smoothing any 3D model in Blender, you might encounter a few problems caused by unmatched face normals. The face normals are the visible side of a face, and depending on the tools and techniques applied to the object, you may have normals facing in opposite directions in an object.

For instance, if you look at the object in Figure 4.10, you will see a dark spot from the smoothing process.

Figure 4.10 - *Object with dark spot*

If you want to see the difference between normals in that object, we can enable the visualization of the face normals in the Overlays menu. That menu is available in the left of your shading options at the 3D Viewport header (Figure 4.11).

Figure 4.11 - *Overlay options*

At the bottom of the menu, you will find the options to display normals for vertex, edge, of faces. Enable the option to display normals for faces and increase the size. Your normals will appear as small perpendicular lines pointing out of the face (Figure 4.12).

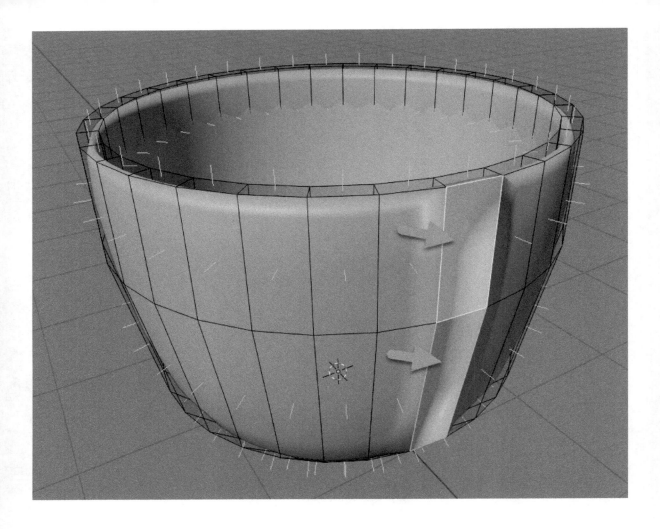

Figure 4.12 - *Normals in object*

You must be in Edit Mode to view and manipulate Normals. As you can see from Figure 4.12, the normals for part of the object are pointing in opposite directions. If you want a smooth surface for any object, all normals must point to the same direction.

You can force the recalculation of normals using the SHIFT+N keys to make Blender point all of them to the outside of a model. Before you press the keys, make sure you select all faces from the object with the A key and then press the SHIFT+N.

As a result, you will get the faces pointing to the outside of the model and a clean, smooth surface (Figure 4.13).

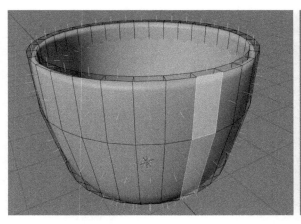 

Figure 4.13 - Clean smooth surface

Whenever you see dark spots at an object surface after you apply a Subdivision Surface modifier and a Shade Smooth, you probably have a problem with the normals. Enable the visualization of normals in the Overlays menu to investigate and apply a fix.

You have additional options to handle normals in the **Mesh → Normals** menu.

*Tip: If you want to invert the normals of a face you can use the Flip option from the **Mesh → Normals** menu.*

4.2.3 Controlling smoothing radius with loops

Once you apply a Subdivision Surface modifier to an object, you will notice that for some shapes it will round the edges and corners or models. The roundness of a model will have a different radius based on the distance between faces.

For instance, if you look at the model shown in Figure 4.14, you will see that it will use a large relative radius for the smoothed version of the model.

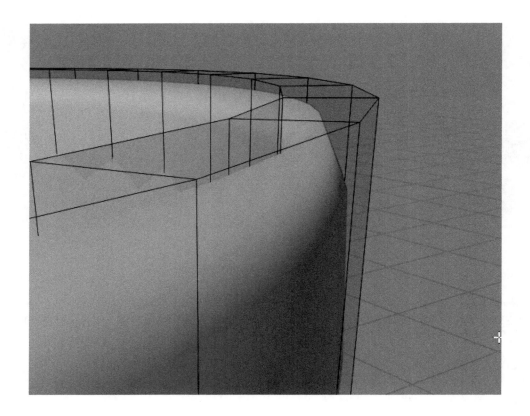

Figure 4.14 - *Radius difference*

You can control the distance you will get for the radius with the Loop Cut tool. By adding new edge loops to shape, you will be able to set the radius size visually. For instance, if we add a new loop to the top of our model with the CTRL+R key and make it stay close to the upper edges (Figure 4.15).

Figure 4.15 - *New loops results*

The result will be a smooth surface with e much smaller radius. Whenever you have a model that receives a Subdivision Surface Modifier, you can use the Loop Cut to control the radius of rounded shapes.

Tip: You can easily select edge loops in Blender by holding the ALT key while you select any edge. Blender will try to select all connected edges in a loop.

4.3 Mirror modifier

In the modifiers list, you will find another essential tool regarding modeling for Blender, which is the Mirror modifier. Unlike the Mirror tool that you can apply using the CTRL+M keys, you will get a copy of your selected object using the Mirror modifier.

To use the modifier, you have to select the object you want to mirror and apply the modifier. At the list of settings, you have to pick an axis to create the mirror copy (Figure 4.16).

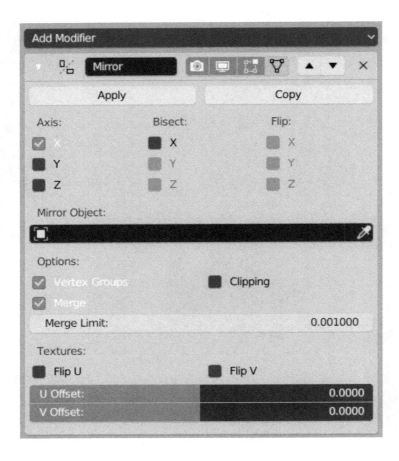

Figure 4.16 - Mirror modifier

Choose the axis, and you will get a mirrored copy of your object with the origin point as the pivot for the copy (Figure 4.17).

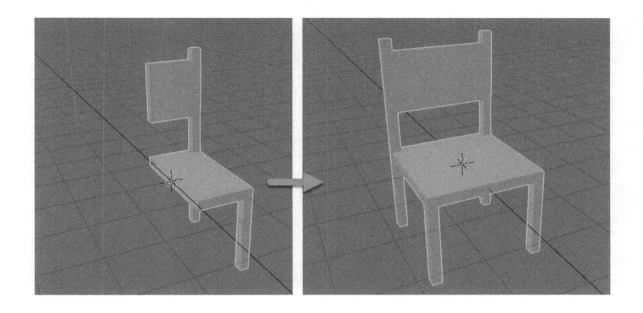

Figure 4.17 - *Mirror results*

As you can see from Figure 4.16, the location of your origin point is critical for any Mirror copy created with the modifier. If your origin point is at a distant location from the object, your copies will also appear with the same distance.

After adding a Mirror modifier to any object, you can make that copy became part of the object by using the Apply button. That will remove the modifier from the list and add the geometry to the object. You can use the Merge option with the Distance settings to merge all vertices from the original object and the copy.

Info: Another option to control if the modifier will connect the copied shape and your original object is the Threshold distance. That distance is usually small, close to zero, and will set the minimum limit for Blender to look for surrounding vertices for merging.

If the object must also receive other modifiers to alter their shape, you can add them before a Mirror. For instance, in Figure 4.18, you can see an object that receives a Subdivision Surface first and then a Mirror.

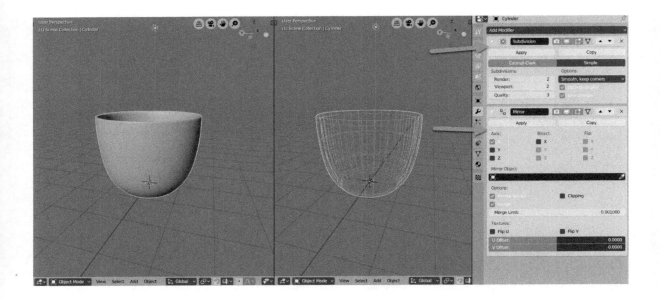

Figure 4.18 - Modifiers order

It will first have a smoothed surface and then a mirrored copy. Always consider the order in which you will use the modifiers to change the surface of an object. In any case, you can change the order of the modifiers using the arrows at the top of each modifier.

4.4 Array modifier

If your model has a pattern that you can repeat multiple times to create the main shape the Array Modifier can help you with the modeling. With the Array, we can get any object copied in a matrix format.

For instance, if we use the form shown in Figure 4.19 and apply an Array Modifier. You will get several copies of that shape repeated side by side.

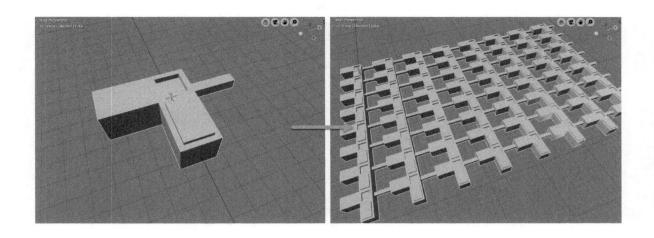

Figure 4.19 - *Shape with Array*

To use an Array for modeling, you will have to select the object first and add the modifier. Once you have the Array Modifier, you see the options to start making copies of the object (Figure 4.20).

Figure 4.20 - *Array options*

At the top, you will see the Count that controls the number of duplicates. There are three main types of copies you can use for the Array:

- **Fixed count**: You will use a relative size for the selected object. For instance, in the distance, you will enter the value two, and it will use two times the size of your object as a distance.

- **Fit length**: Here, you will get absolute distances. If you use a value of 2, the copies will stay at two units from each other regardless of the object size.

- **Fit Curve**: You can also use a curve object to control the size. You can create a curve with the SHIFT+A keys and choose the Curve group.

After you choose the method you want to use for the copies, it is time to pick the values and axis used for the copies. For instance, in the X field, you can set the value used for copies in the X-axis. If you use a value of 1 for the X and 3 for Count, you will get five copies in the X-axis. Using the Fixed Count type, they will repeat three times in the X-axis (Figure 4.21).

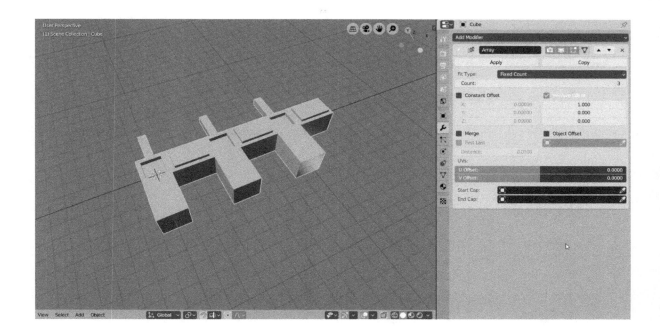

Figure 4.21 - *Copies in the X-axis*

A single Array Modifier will only make copies of a single row or column of objects if you imagine the result as a matrix. You will need two Arrays to get a bi-dimensional pattern. For instance, we can use one Array for the X-axis and other for the Y-axis (Figure 4.22).

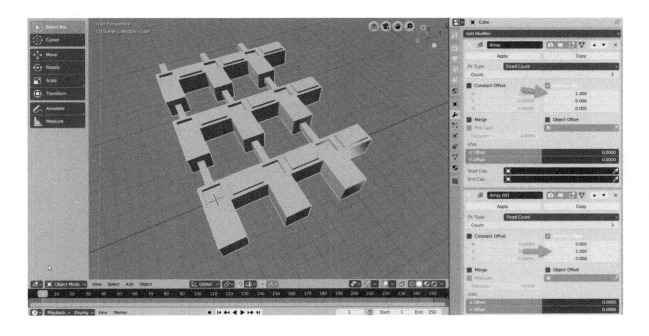

Figure 4.22 - *Copies with two Arrays*

That is the easiest way to get a matrix style set of copies.

4.4.1 Arrays and reference objects

Besides using values to control the distance of an Array, you can also use an object to set ranges and even rotations for an Array. It could be an existing 3d Model from your scene or a helper object like an Empty from Blender.

The Empty is a unique object in Blender that will not appear in rendering but work only as a reference for modeling, animation, or any other task that requires an object.

You can create an Empty using the SHIFT+A key and choose Empty with the option Plain Axis for the most straightforward type of Empty (Figure 4.23).

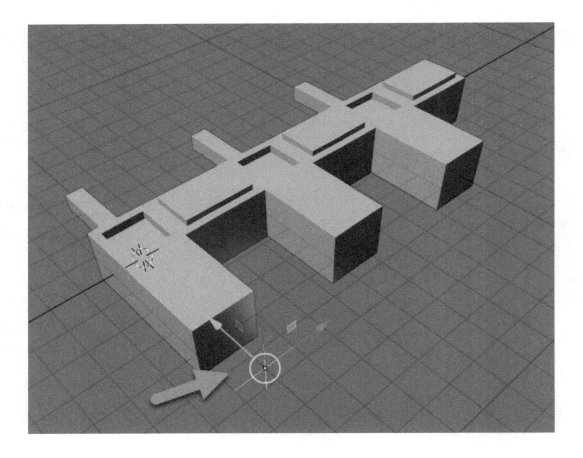

Figure 4.23 - *Empty object*

How can an Empty help us with an Array? At the Array options, you will see a field called Offset object. We can use any object from the scene in Blender as the Offset object, which will control the Array distance, rotation, and scaling.

For instance, if you have an existing Array and add an Empty to the Object offset field, it will immediately take control of your Array. If you rotate and move the Empty around, you will create unique shapes using the Array (Figure 4.24).

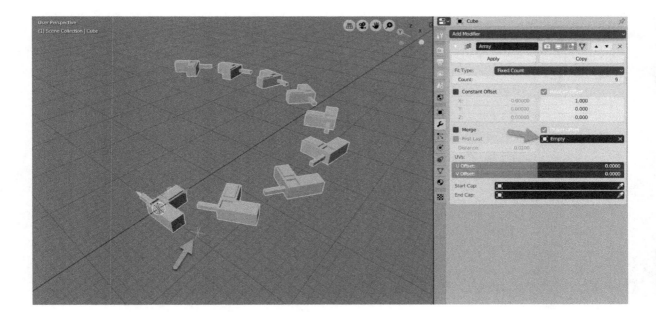

Figure 4.24 - *Array with Empty*

Once you click at the Object offset in the Array options, you will see a list with all the object names in your scene. Choose the name for the Empty, which will probably be Empty.

If you add some animation data to the Empty, it will be possible to create interesting abstract animations using the Array. You will learn more about animation with Blender in chapter 7.

Tip: *Remember that you can easily rename any object in your project using the F3 key. Select the object and press the key to assign a new name.*

4.5 Boolean modifier

Another modifier that will be useful for modeling projects is the Boolean, which will allow you to create models based on interactions between objects. The modifier will create new shapes based on:

– Intersections

127

– Subtractions

– Unions

You can get 3D objects from those interactions that would be hard to create as a single model. For most of the operations, you will need at least two objects, which you will have to select by name.

One of the most typical uses of the Boolean Modifier is to open round holes in 3D objects. You will need an object that you want to modify and a cylinder. Place the cylinder at the same location where you want to open the hole (Figure 4.25).

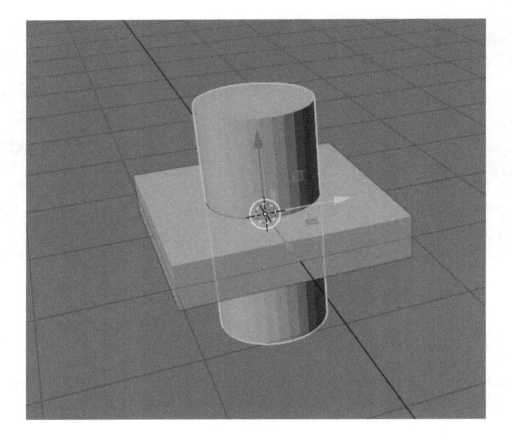

Figure 4.25 - Objects for Boolean

After you place the objects, you can apply the Boolean modifier to the object that will receive the hole. You will set the operation to Difference to subtract the shape of another object, and add the cylinder as the second object (Figure 4.26).

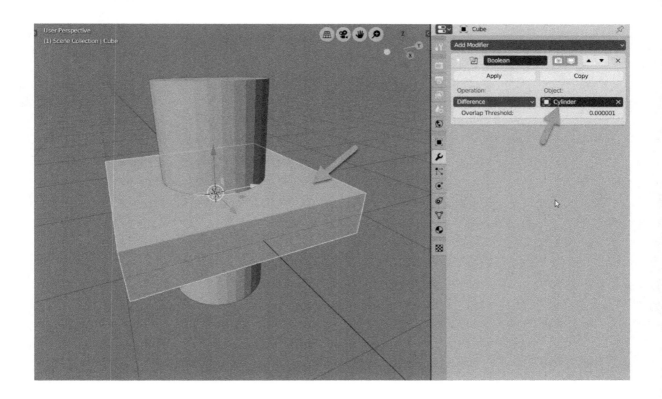

Figure 4.26 - Boolean settings

At first, you will not notice any changes to the object, because the Boolean will apply the hole in real-time. You must press the Apply button to make the modification permanent, and after moving the base object, you will see the hole with the same shape of your cylinder (Figure 4.27).

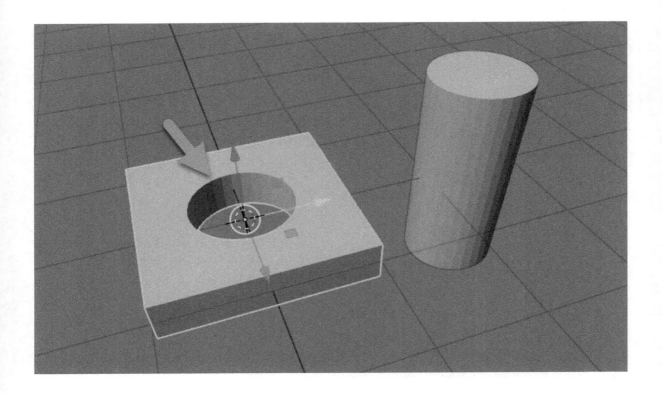

Figure 4.27 - Boolean results

The Union option will create a new shape based on the merge of two existing objects, and with the Intersect, you will get a new shape based on the shared space between two objects.

4.6 Spin tool for rounded shapes

For the cases where you need parts of a model to have perfectly rounded shapes, it will be hard to use only an extrude to create the model. In Blender, we have a tool called Spin that can help in making perfect round shapes. The Spin works like an extrude that will happen in a curve.

As a result, you will get an arch shape for the selected object. Using the Spin is easy if you know the rules to create the shape:

- The Spin uses the 3D Cursor as the pivot point for the rotation and arch center.

- You must activate the Spin with a perpendicular view from your rotation.

- Use the small menu on the lower left of your 3D Viewport to control the segmentation and angle for the Spin.

- Control the direction of the Spin with positive or negative values for the Angle.

In Figure 4.28, you can see an example of what you can create using the Spin.

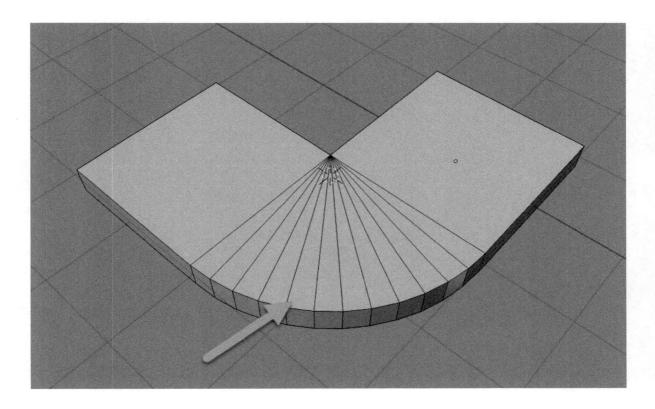

Figure 4.28 - *Rounded shape from the Spin*

To use the Spin, you have to go into Edit Mode and select the parts of your model that it must replicate during while applying the rotation. For instance, we can take the face from a shape like the one shown in Figure 4.29.

Figure 4.29 - *Face for the Spin*

Once you have the selected elements, which could be either a set of edges or vertices, it is time to place the 3D Cursor. Move the 3D Cursor location to the point you wish to use as the pivot in your Spin rotation (Figure 4.30).

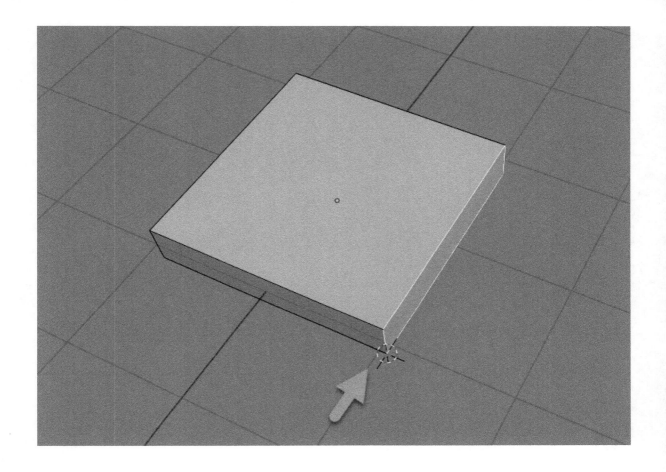

Figure 4.30 - *3D Cursor location*

The easiest way to move your 3D Cursor to that location is by using the Snap tool. Before you trigger the Spin from the Toolbar of your 3D Viewport, you must set the view you have from the object to the top. Press the seven key on your Numpad.

When in the top view, you can press the Spin button. A blue arc will appear close to the selected elements. Click and drag your mouse above the arch, and you will start to see your round shape appearing. At the Spin options that will appear on the lower-left corner, you can control the rotation and steps used by the rounded shape (Figure 4.31).

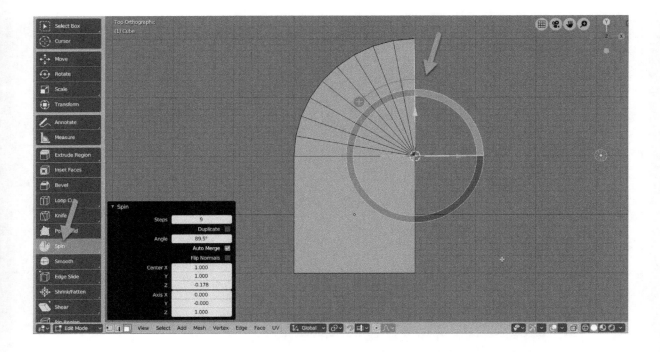

Figure 4.31 - Spin shape

Make sure you get all the options and settings for the Spin right after you create the rounded shape because the menu will disappear after you start another tool in Blender.

In the Spin menu, you will also find an option called "Dupli" that will not connect the copies generated by the Spin. It will work like a rotation based Array.

4.7 Proportional editing

The transformations we apply to any object in Blender will take full effect on all selected objects, but they will not influence the surrounding elements. For instance, if you choose a couple of vertices from a polygon that has hundreds of vertices, you will apply the transformations only to those selected.

What if you also wanted to apply transformations to those other vertices with a lower force? You can do that in Blender using the Proportional Editing tools. The option is available at the 3D Viewport header, and you can choose the enable it with the O key (Figure 4.32).

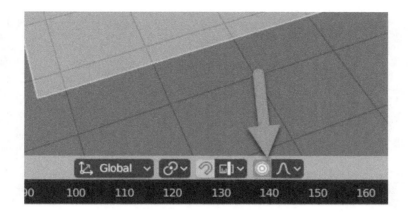

Figure 4.32 - Proportional editing tools

If you enable the tool, you will have to choose a falloff type from the options right next to the icon where you enable the Proportional Editing tools (Figure 4.33).

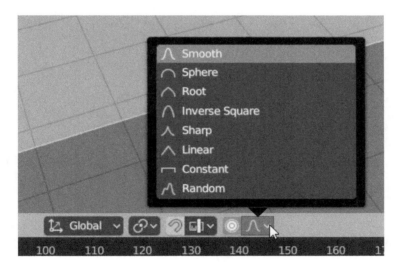

Figure 4.33 - Fallout types

By enabling the tool and using as a fallout type the smoothing option, you can select a single vertex from a plane with multiple subdivisions, and start move transformation in the Z-axis. As a result, you will get the surrounding vertices also moving up (Figure 4.34).

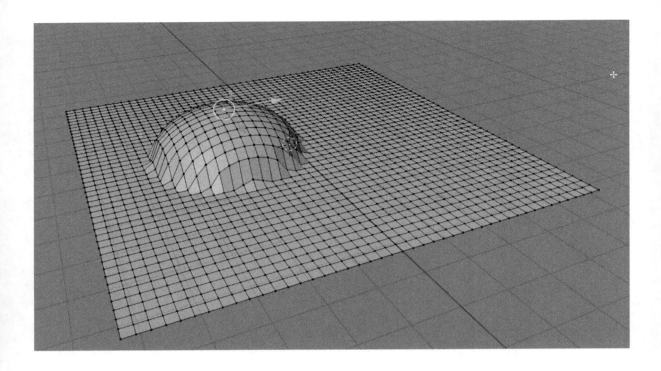

Figure 4.34 - *Proportional editing vertices*

You will notice that a small circle will appear around the selected vertice showing the area of influence for the proportional editing. It is possible to increase or decrease the influence using the mouse wheel or the plus and minus keys from your Numpad.

By the way, you create a plane like the one shown in Figure 4.34 with the Context menu. Select the plane and go to Edit Mode. In Edit Mode, press the A key to select all vertices and with a right-click open the Context menu.

There you will choose the first option called Subdivision. For each time you choose the Subdivision, you will get the edges of a model divided once. Apply multiple of those Subdivisions to get a high-density mesh.

What is next?

The next step to improve or projects in Blender is applying materials and textures to the objects you create. By using materials, we can give a visual context to objects and highly increase the realism of 3D models. In Blender, you will find several controls that will allow you to create realistic materials.

You will learn how to apply and manage materials for rendering in the next chapter. There we will learn how to use textures that work in both Eevee and Cycles.

From simple materials that use a standard shader, you will jump to PBR materials that use composition from multiple textures to create realistic surfaces. You will learn all the tools required to start making materials for your projects.

Chapter 5 - Materials and textures

Using materials as textures is a crucial component for any project, and in this chapter, you will learn how to manage and apply materials, textures, and shaders to objects. You will find a dedicated material editor in Blender and also a special type of editor for something called Nodes.

The Nodes will give you a lot of flexibility and power to craft all kinds of materials and use one that can transform your scenes. With PBR materials and Nodes, you will be ready to create realistic images using Blender.

You will learn how to use and find some high-quality PBR materials for your projects.

Here is a list of what you will learn:

- Apply materials to objects
- Manage and rename materials
- Protect materials from the purge process with a Fake user
- Choose the best shader for a material
- Use image textures
- Control projection and tilling for textures
- Apply PBR materials to objects
- Use Nodes to control and craft materials
- Apply glossy and transparent shaders to objects
- Use multiple materials for the same object

5.1 Adding materials to objects

Any scene in Blender will benefit from a good lighting setup and also materials that will give meaning to surfaces. The materials in Blender will provide you with plenty of tools and options to assign textures and other effects to create a visual context for surfaces.

For instance, if you have to create a surface that should appear as a stone wall, you can use a texture on that object to make it look like a stone wall. With materials, we can create all types of surfaces based on a combination of shaders, effects, and textures.

Before we start to deal with material creation and shaders, it is essential to define a few aspects of materials in Blender:

– Materials exist in Blender assigned to an object.

– You can remove material from an object, and Blender will purge a material that no objects are using. The purge will occur when you close Blender.

– Multiple objects can use the same material.

– Each material can receive a unique name that will help you identify what it represents visually.

– You can reuse materials in other projects using the Append and Link options from the File menu.

To create a material in Blender, you have to select an object first and then go to the Material tab at the Properties Editor (Figure 5.1).

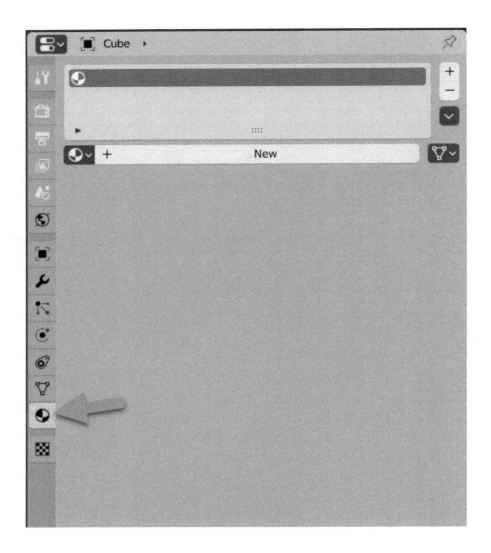

Figure 5.1 - *Material tab*

At the Material tab, you will either see a button that will allow you to create new material or a list with options to edit existing material.

For objects that already have a material, you will see all the controls available to manage the material at the top of this tab (Figure 5.2).

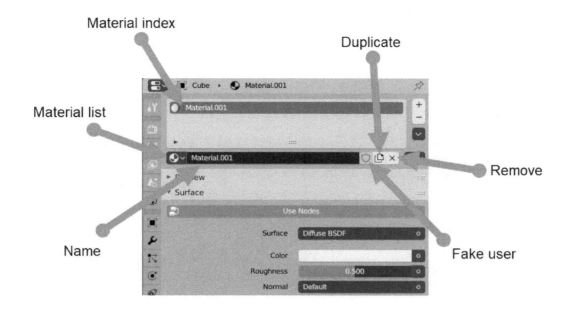

Figure 5.2 - Material controls

Here is a list with what you can do with each of the controls:

- **Name**: In the text field you can rename the material. It is important to assign meaningful names for materials, which will help you later identify what they represent.

- **Remove**: With this button, you can remove the material from the object. It won't erase the material. If it doesn't have any objects assigned Blender will purge the material the next time you exit the software.

- **Duplicate**: In some cases, you may want to create a new material using another one as a template. With the duplicate button, you can create a copy of existing material.

- **Fake user**: Any material that doesn't have an object assigned will be at risk of deletion when you close Blender. You can enable the Fake User that will keep any material from getting purged, even if it doesn't have any objects assigned.

- **Material list**: All your materials will become part of the Blender file you are working. Using this button will list all materials available in this file, and you can easily reuse any of them. Instead of creating new material, you can select an object and pick one from this list. The list is also useful to show materials that don't have any objects assigned. You will see the number zero right next to a material that doesn't have any objects assigned.

- **Material index**: We can have multiple materials in a single object with the use of indexes. Here you have a list of all materials assigned for each index in the object.

Using these controls will make your management of materials a lot easier and allow you to reuse existing materials.

Info: Most of the materials options will work the same regardless of the renderer you choose.

5.2 Material editor and shaders

After you create material for any object, the first thing you will do is choose a proper shader for that material. A shader is one of the most important elements of any material because it will determine how the object will interact with light. You can have a material that behaves like glass or an opaque surface.

What will set the behavior of your material is the shader you choose from the list of available options (Figure 5.3).

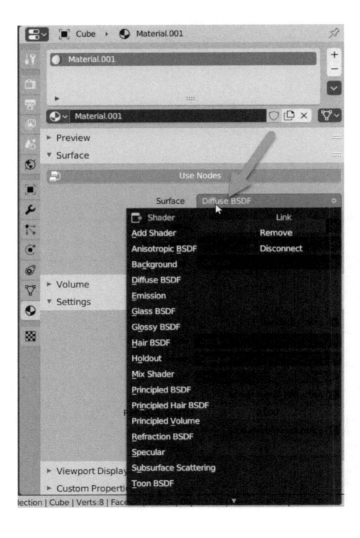

Figure 5.3 - *Shader list for Blender*

From the list you will find some shaders like:

- **Diffuse BSDF**: A simple shader that will create an opaque surface absorbing all light.
- **Glossy BSDF**: The shader you will want to use for surfaces that have any level of reflection like mirrors and some types of metals.
- **Glass BSDF**: If you need realistic transparency you will use the Glass BSDF for advanced reflections and light distortion.
- **Emission**: A material that will behave like a light source and contribute to the lighting of a scene.
- **Mix Shader**: With this option, you can blend multiple shaders to create unique effects.
- **Transparent BSDF**: If you need simple transparency in materials, you will use the Transparent BSDF.
- **Principled BSDF**: A powerful shader that can create most of the effects alone and will be the base for all surfaces using physically-based materials.

To use any of the shaders, you will have to select one from the list available at the location shown in Figure 5.3. Once you pick a shader, it will be time to set up all the details about the surface. Some shaders will offer simple controls like the Diffuse BSDF that will let you choose a color.

Info: *The BSDF acronym means Bidirectional Scattering Distribution Function, which identifies the mathematical function that controls how a surface scatter light.*

Others like the Principled BSDF will feature a full list of settings that we will discuss in more detail at section 5.4 PBR texture in Blender.

If you have to create a material that has a simple color, add the Diffuse BSDF to the material. From the color picker, you will be able to get the color you want (Figure 5.4).

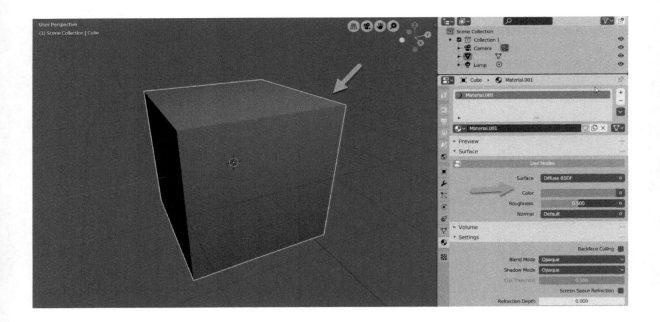

Figure 5.4 - *Diffuse BSDF material*

You can preview the material in two locations:

1. At the Material tab, you will see a Preview field that will display the materials in a geometrical primitive.
2. You can also use the 3D Viewport by choosing the Rendered shading mode. Press the Z key and choose Rendered. For real-time previews, you can make use you are using Eevee for rendering. That is the default renderer for Blender. Even if you are using Cycles later, you can use Eevee for fast material previews.

The Material tab will show all the important options in a vertical list for editing aspects of your surfaces. However, you should also use the Shader Editor to have much better flexibility for material creation.

5.2.1 The Shader Editor

When you are working on material for an object that requires multiple shaders, textures, and other effects, you will get a limited view from the Material tab vertical display. To have more flexibility and power regarding material setup, you should use the Shader Editor.

That is a special type of Editor in Blender that will display data in a workflow style using Nodes for information like Shaders. With the Shader Editor, you will have options to edit not only materials but also your environment and even post-processing effects for render.

To open the Shader Editor, you can either use a WorkSpace for shading or swap an existing division in your interface with the Shader Editor. For instance, you can use the Timeline area from the default user interface and open a Shader Editor (Figure 5.5).

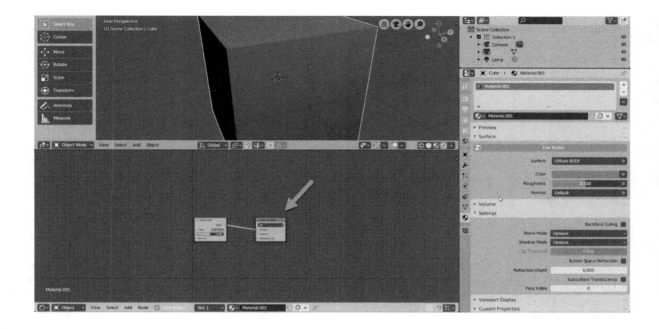

Figure 5.5 - *Shader Editor*

With the Shader Editor, you will see blocks of information for materials that receive the name of Node. You will connect Nodes like a workflow of information. For materials, you always have the last Node as the "Material Output" and what comes before this Node will depend on the material you create.

A few important facts about Nodes:

– Each Node could have input and output sockets that are those circles on the side of each Node. For instance, you will see Shaders having both input and output. The "Material Output" Node only have input sockets.

– The sockets have color codes that identify what type of data they can handle.

– You can connect Nodes by clicking and dragging from an output socket to an input.

– To select and manipulate Nodes, you can use the same shortcuts from the 3D Viewport.

– To break a connection, you can hold the CTRL key while clicking and dragging with the right mouse button. The cursor will turn to a knife, and you will be able to cut connections.

– You can erase a Node with either the X key or DEL.

– To create new Nodes, you can use the SHIFT+A key or the Add menu in the Shader Editor.

A simple example of what we can do with the Shader Editor is with the Mix Shader that will allow us to blend two different shaders for a single material. We can mix a Diffuse BSDF and a Glossy BSDF:

1. Select an object and add new material.

2. Choose the Diffuse BSDF as the Shader.

3. Open the Shader Editor

4. Press the SHIFT+A keys, and from the Shaders group add a Mix Shader

5. Press the SHIFT+A again, and from the Shaders group add a Glossy BSDF

You will get the Nodes shown in Figure 5.6.

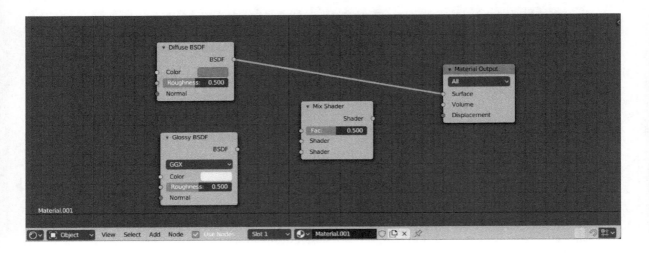

Figure 5.6 - *Nodes with no connections*

Now, we have to rearrange the Nodes to make both the Diffuse BSDF and Glossy BSDF connect to the Mix Shader. The Mix Shader will connect to the Material Output.

To connect the Nodes, we have two options:

– You can break the connection from the Diffuse BSDF to the Material Output by holding the CTRL key while clicking and dragging with the right mouse button. Click and drag from the output sockets of the Diffuse and Glossy to the Mix Shader. Connect the Mix Shader to the Material Output.

– Since the Diffuse BSDF already have a connection to the Material Output, move the Mix Shader Node until it is above the connection line between the Diffuse BSDF and Material Output. You will see the line becoming highlighted, and if you release the Mix Shader, it will rearrange the connections and stay between both Nodes. You can connect the Glossy BSDF to the Mix Shader.

Both options will produce the same result, which you can see in Figure 5.7.

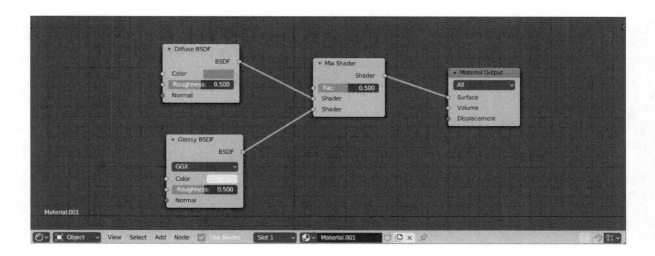

Figure 5.7 - *Material results with the Mix Shader*

The handling of all other Nodes and materials will use similar settings and procedures. By the way, you can do the same thing with the Material tab. From the Shaders list, you can choose the Mix Shader (Figure 5.8).

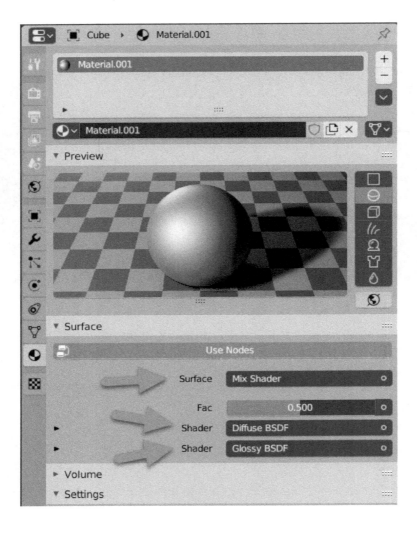

Figure 5.8 - Mix Shader

In the Mix Shader, you can select the two different Shaders that will compose the material. You have the option to use either the Material tab or Shader Editor. The advantage of using the Shader Editor is that it works more visually and will give you an edge when using complex materials with several Nodes.

5.3 Using image textures

Using the Shaders alone won't produce realistic results for some materials, where an image texture will be the best choice. To add an image texture to any material, you will use a Node called "Image Texture."

Info: From this point forward, we will use mainly the Shader Editor to craft materials. But, you will get the same results with the Material tab.

To add the Node to the material, you will press the SHIFT+A key in the Shader Editor or use the Add menu. Go to the Texture group and choose Image Texture (Figure 5.9).

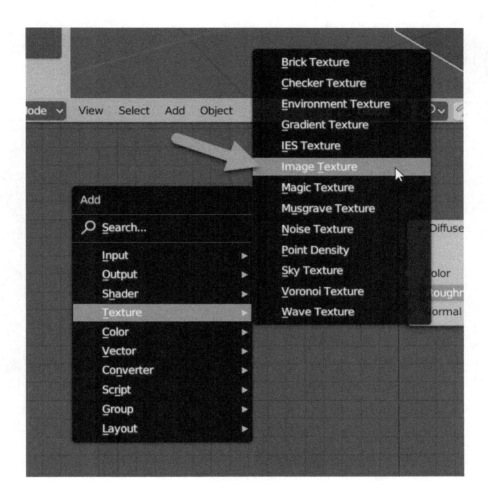

Figure 5.9 - *Image Texture*

From the Node, you will click on the "Open" button and pick an image file from your hard drive. After you open the texture file, you will connect the Node to the input socket of your Diffuse BSDF (Figure 5.10).

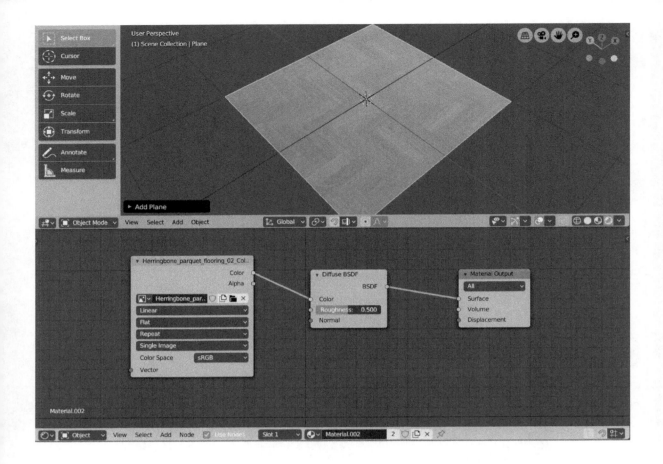

Figure 5.10 - *Image Texture*

The result will be a texture assigned to the material. Any Shader that has an input socket receiving color data will be able to connect with the Image Texture Node.

5.3.1 Projection for image textures

Each image that you use in a material will have an option for the projection, which will affect the way it appears in any object. The projection options are available at the Image Texture Node, and by default will always start as "Flat." That means your image will look good on bidimensional surfaces like planes (Figure 5.11).

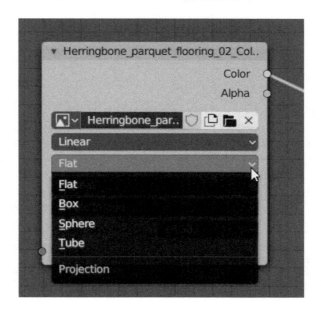

Figure 5.11 - *Projection options*

However, using that projection option in shapes that have depth might result in distortions. You can choose other types of mapping options that can match the shape of multiple objects. A common choice for 3D models with textures is the "Box" that will consider the depth of an object (Figure 5.12).

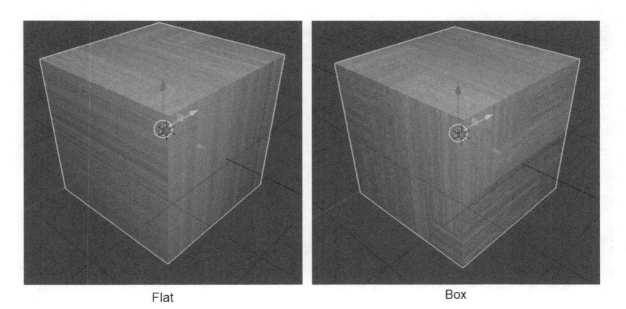

Flat   Box

Figure 5.12 - *Box projection*

For the cases where you have a spherical or cylindrical 3D model, you can use the other two mapping options Sphere and Cylinder respectively.

5.3.2 Tilling for image textures

After you have a texture assigned to any material, you will probably want to have additional controls on how the image appears on a surface. Usually, you will have an image with a repeating pattern that will cover a large surface. The technique has a name of tilling.

Unless you add controls that generate that tilling effect the image texture will not repeat on a surface. To create the tilling effect, you will need two additional Nodes:

– From the Input → Texture Coordinates

– From the Vector → Mapping

You will connect the Generated output socket from the Texture Coordinates to the Mapping. From the Mapping, you will connect it to the Image Texture (Figure 5.13).

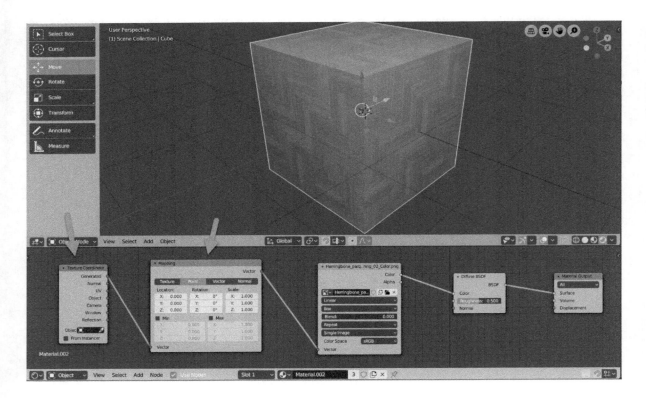

Figure 5.13 - Tilling controls

To control the tilling of textures, we will use the Scale field from the Mapping Node. If you increase the size for the scale, the Mapping will multiply the textures in the same region. For instance, using a scale of two for all axis in a Cube will result in two textures side by side in all axis (Figure 5.14).

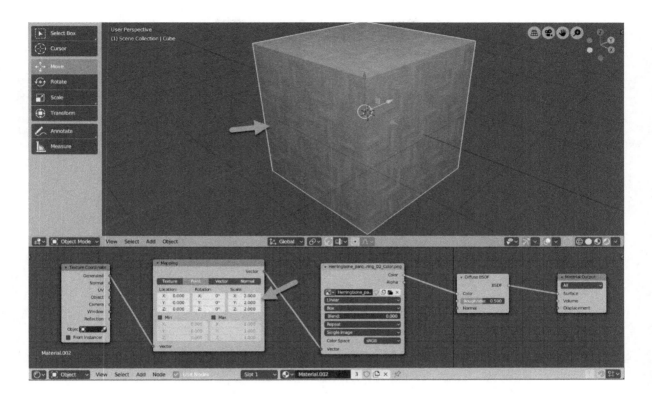

Figure 5.14 - Texture tilling

If you want to increase the size of your textures, you can use smaller values like "0.5" that will cut in half the size of your textures.

Tip: To use textures with tilling you should always look for seamless texture images. Those textures won't show visible borders when placed side by side.

5.4 PBR textures in Blender

For projects where you need maximum realism for materials in Blender, you will have to use a special type of material called PBR. The acronym means "Physically Based Render" and identifies a material that has multiple textures. Each texture in the material has a purpose of representing a feature of the material.

Usually, a simple PBR texture will feature textures for:

- Color (Diffuse)

- Roughness

- Normal (Bump)

You will connect each one of the maps to the input sockets of a Shader, and they will produce a realistic surface. The Shader you will use for PBR materials is the Principled BSDF (Figure 5.15).

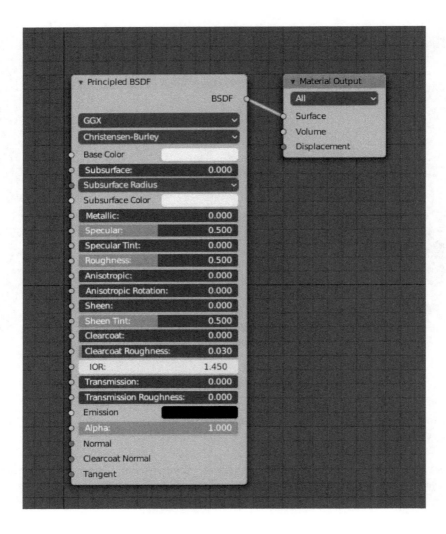

Figure 5.15 - Principled BSDF

Before we start to use PBR materials, you will have to find some of those special sets of textures. Several online libraries offer free PBR materials. Two of the best are:

- cc0textures.com

- texturehaven.com

They provide high-quality PBR textures in public domain with resolutions going up to 8k (8.192 pixels). You will download textures from those libraries as a compacted zip file. After extracting those files to your hard drive, you will get multiple image files with a suffix identifying the type of map (Figure 5.16).

Bricks18_col.jpg   Bricks18_disp.jpg   Bricks18_nrm.jpg   Bricks18_rgh.jpg

Figure 5.16 - *PBR material files*

To set up a PBR material, you will create new material and choose the Principles BSDF as the shader. Add an Image Texture Node by pressing the SHIFT+A key in the Shader Editor. You can also drag and drop the image file from your file manager to the Shader Editor.

In that case, Blender will automatically create the Image Texture Node. For the remaining Image Texture Nodes, you can select the first Node and press the SHIFT+D keys to duplicate it twice. Or drag and drop the remaining image textures to the Shader Editor (Figure 5.17).

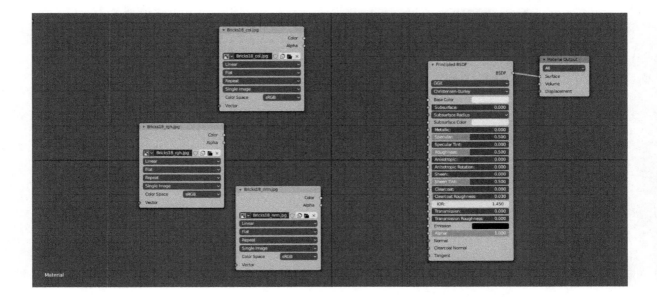

Figure 5.17 - Image Textures

For this example, we will use a PBR material with a Normal map. The Normal and Roughness maps don't affect colors, and for that reason, you should change the color space settings to "Non-Color" (Figure 5.18).

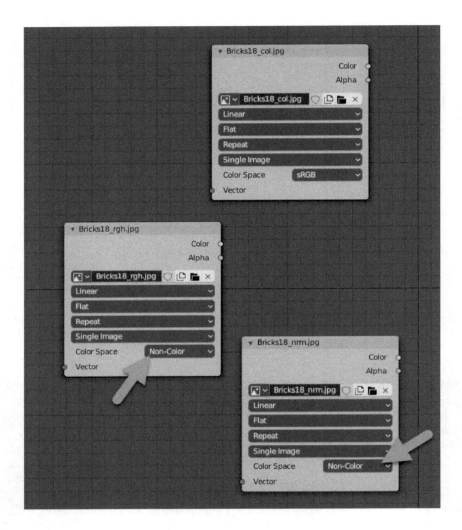

Figure 5.18 - Color Settings

After you set the color settings, we can start connecting the Image Texture Nodes to the Principled BSDF:

1. Connect the Color textures to the Base Color

2. Connect the Roughness texture to the Roughness

For the Normal Texture, we need an additional Node, which you can create from the Vector group. Add a Normal Map Node:

1. Connect the Normal texture to the Normal Map

2. Connect the Normal Map to the Normal

In the end, you should have a Node setup like Figure 5.19 shows.

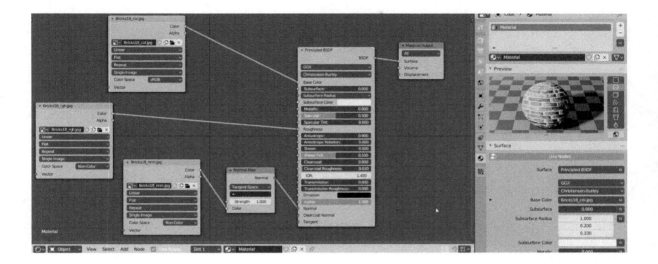

Figure 5.19 - *PBR material with maps*

With the Normal Map Node, it is possible to control the direction of your Bump. For instance, using negative values will invert the ridges created by the map.

You can also add tilling control to the PBR material with the Texture Coordinate and Mapping. Connect the Mapping to each one of the Image Textures for full control (Figure 5.20).

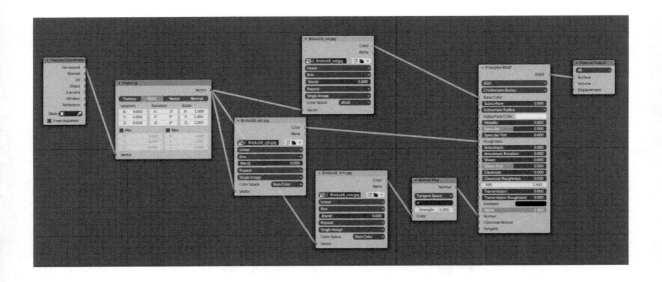

Figure 5.20 - Tilling control

In some textures, you will also find additional maps like Displacement and AO (Ambient Occlusion). Those maps will connect with specific input sockets for the Principled BSDF.

The Ambient Occlusion will connect to the Base Color, where you will need to use a MixRGB Node from the Color group to blend it with the color map (Figure 5.21). For the MixRGB, you should use the Multiply option.

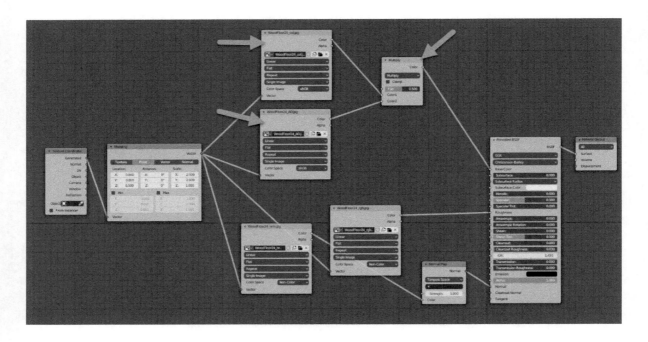

Figure 5.21 - *Ambient Occlusion map*

Most of the PBR materials will offer the same types of maps regarding textures, and with a Principled BSDF, you will be able to create those materials easily. You can even make a template material with all the Nodes prepared to receive your image textures.

5.5 Transparent and glass materials

For materials that require transparency, you can use options like the Glass BSDF and Transparency BSDF. With the Transparency BSDF, you will get materials with a simple effect that doesn't divert light (Figure 5.22).

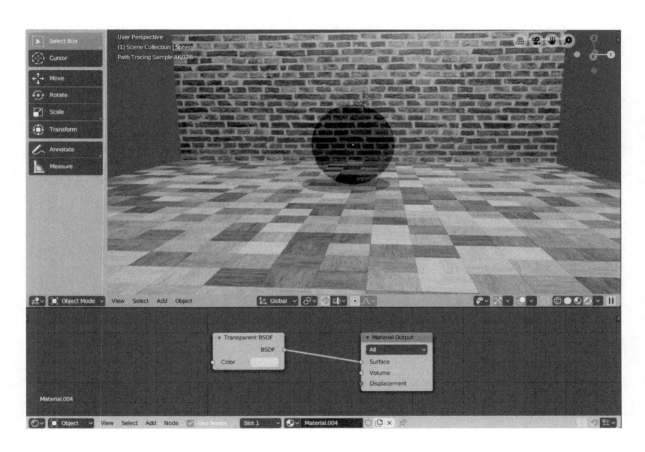

Figure 5.22 - *Transparent BSDF (Cycles)*

In case you need more sophisticated transparency, you should pick the Glass BSDF. The shader has two settings that will help you achieve a more realistic effect:

 – **IOR**: An index that controls the refraction of light.

– **Roughness**: Here, you can control the smoothness of your surface reflection. Values close to zero will create a polish glass surface, and higher values will make it look grainy.

A material with the Glass BSDF can produce great results with transparency (Figure 5.23).

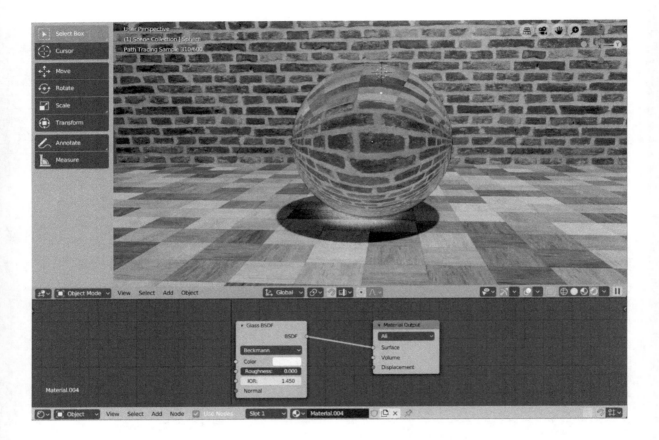

Figure 5.23 - Glass BSDF (Cycles)

Use the IOR settings to control how the light will divert from the interior of your model using a material that has a Glass BSDF. You can also mix the shader with other materials to achieve unique effects with transparency.

5.6 Glossy surfaces

If you want a surface that has a certain level of reflection, you will have to use either a Glossy BSDF or the Principled BSDF. Both shaders feature the main setting that controls how your material will reflect light, which is the roughness.

A material that has a roughness close to zero will have a perfect reflection, almost like a mirror. For higher values, it will start to get a blurred reflection until you cant identify the objects reflected anymore (Figure 5.24).

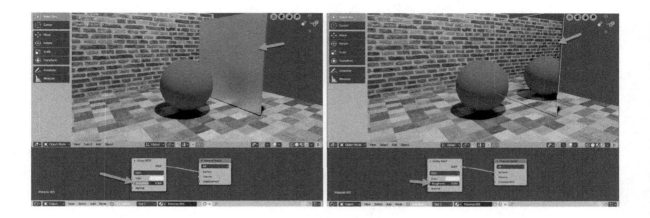

Figure 5.24 - *Glossy surfaces*

If you want a perfect mirror in a material, you will set the Roughness to zero and the color from the Glossy BSDF as black.

5.7 Attaching textures to the Blender file

The textures you add to any material in Blender will be external resources from your main project file. You will have to handle them using the file manager of your system. For instance, if you want to back up the project files to an external hard drive or sent it to a cloud drive, the texture files must also go to the same location.

After you add the textures to a material, they will either have a relative or absolute path to the Blender file. As a good practice, you should always create a unique folder for your project. In that folder, you will save the Blender file alongside all other resources like textures.

It will make the handling of external data easier for large projects and if you have to move the project file somewhere else.

An easy way to avoid all that trouble is with the attachment of your external files to the Blender project file. You can do that with the **File → External Data** menu (Figure 5.25).

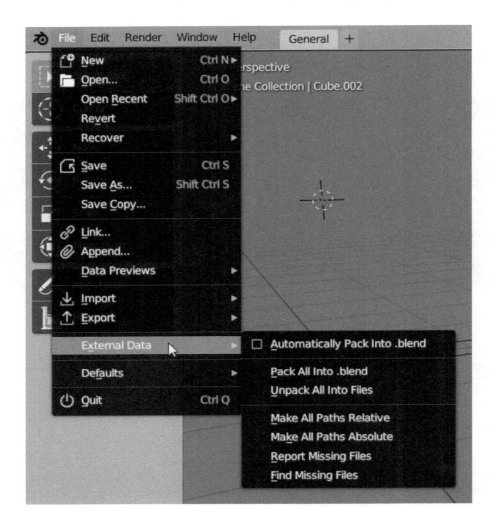

Figure 5.25 - External data options

There you will find an option called "Pack All Into .blend" that will attach all external resources to the Blender project file.

Info: An external file that has a path starting with "//" has a relative path and will most likely come from the same folder of your project file.

You won't have to worry about external files anymore, because the textures will now be part of your project file. However, it may significantly increase the size of your project file. If you have a project file with 1MB in size and 300 of textures, the new project file size will be 301MB.

As a way to make the packing of external data automatic, you can enable the "Automatically Pack All Into .blend." Use the "Unpack All Into Files" to extract the files to your project folder.

There is also an option to unpack texture files right next to the image filename individually. At the Image Texture Node, you will see a button called Unpack Item (Figure 5.26).

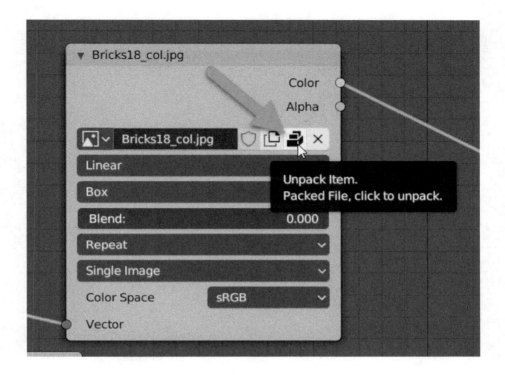

Figure 5.26 - *Unpack item*

Press this icon to extract one image file to the project folder.

Tip: *When Blender can't find a texture file, it will show a pink color instead of the texture. The visual code represents an error where a file is missing. You will have to replace the texture to fix that pink color, which could appear in material or any other location where you can insert texture files.*

5.8 Using multiple materials

What if you want to apply multiple materials in the same object? When you have that type of object that must receive multiple materials, we will have to use the indexes available at the top of your material editor.

To show how you can use multiple materials with the same object, we can use a simple model like the one shown in Figure 5.27.

Figure 5.27 - *Model with multiple faces*

You can make an object like this one with a plane. In Edit Mode, select all vertices and with a right-click open the Context menu. Choose the Subdivide option a few times to create multiple divisions.

At your Material tab, you will see a few extra options when you select any object and go to Edit Mode. You will find buttons bellow your indexes for Assign, Select, and Deselect (Figure 5.28).

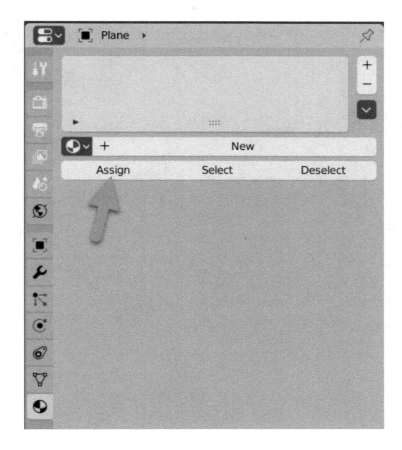

Figure 5.28 - *Material tab in Edit Mode*

For instance, if you create red material using a Diffuse BSDF shader for the first index and select half of the faces for the object. You can press the Assign button after you select the material (Figure 5.29).

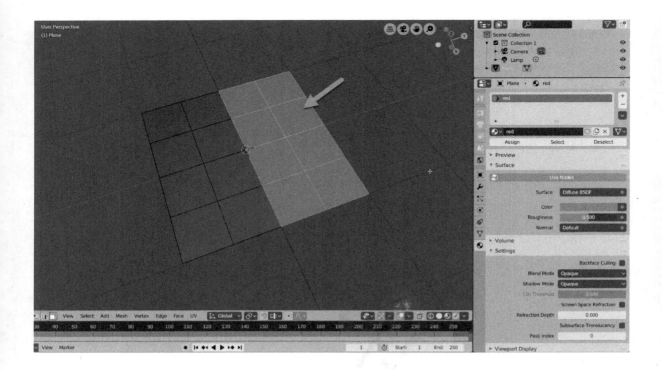

Figure 5.29 - Red material

That will make those faces use the material for the index with the red material. Add another index for that object using the "+" button on the right. Select an existing material or create a new one from scratch. In our case, we can create a simple material called "green" with a Diffuse BSDF shader and a green color.

Select the other half of your object faces and with the index containing the "green" material selected, press the Assign button (Figure 5.30).

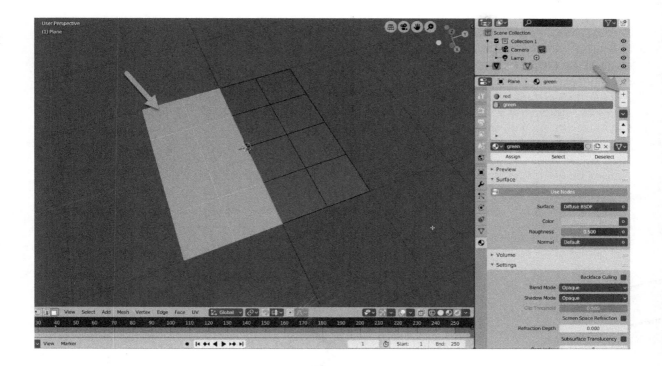

Figure 5.30 - *Green material*

By the end, you will have an object using two materials. If you need more materials for the object, you can keep adding new indexes and selecting other parts of the model. Mark the elements you want to use and press the Assign button.

What is next?

After adding materials to objects, we are ready for the next step in any project related to 3D visualization, which is rendering and illumination. In Blender, you will find two renderers available to generate either still images or animations.

Using Eevee or Cycles, you will be able to create quick real-time renders from any projects at the cost of realism. Or use Cycles to get photo-real images that might take hours or days to render.

The next chapter will teach you about the render selection and illumination process of scenes using Eevee and Cycles. They share some settings for materials, but lights must receive a few unique adjustments for each renderer.

Chapter 6 - Rendering and illumination

The rendering and illumination of any scene are for many artists; one of the most challenging aspects of any project you develop in Blender. To make thing even more complicated, you will have to choose between two render engines.

In the following chapter, you will learn how to choose between Cycles and Eevee and set up lights and a render. You will see the full process to set up the same scene using both render engines, which will give you a great idea of how they work.

Besides rendering, you will also learn more about shading and camera setup.

Here is a list of what you will learn:

– Differences between Eevee and Cycles

– How to choose Eevee or Cycles for rendering

– Use shading modes for render

– Control and adjust the camera

– Adjust the focal length from cameras

– Saving renders as images

– Using environment maps

– Add lights to the scene

– Setup a project using Eevee and Cycles

6.1 Rendering and shading modes

Once you have a 3D model with materials and textures, the next step is trying to get a render from your project. To render a project in Blender, you will have first to decide which is the render engine you will want to use. Nowadays we have two options to render in Blender:

- Eevee

- Cycles

They both are great renderers that are useful in specific types of projects. You will use Cycles for projects that demand light accuracy and cutting-edge realism. All this quality from Cycles has a high cost in terms of computational power.

Usually, we will get longer render times with Cycles, which could range from a couple of hours to days for a render. It will depend on several factors like the complexity of your scene and the hardware used to render.

Eevee is the new renderer that appeared with Blender 2.8 and is capable of working with real-time visualization. The technology behind Eevee is closer to what we find in modern 3D games, where you will see a less realistic solution for lights and materials but with incredible speed.

You will choose between Eevee and Cycles at the Render tab in your Properties Editor (Figure 6.1).

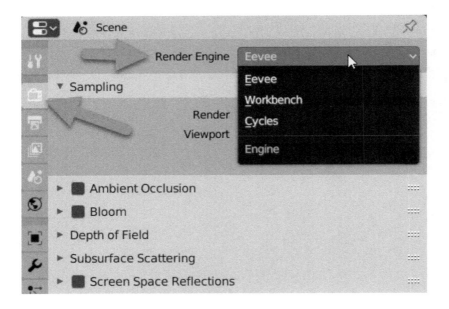

Figure 6.1 - *Render engine selector*

By default, you will always start with Eevee as the main render engine, but you can change it to Cycles at any moment.

Should you always choose Eevee or Cycles for rendering? That will depend on your main objective for a project. Here is a quick summary between them:

- **Cycles**: Easier to set up and get realistic results, but will require you several minutes or hours to get a finished image.

- **Eevee**: Deliver results in real-time but will not get the same level of realism from Cycles, and will require some work to find the best settings.

For materials and lights preview you can quickly go with Eevee and swap later to Cycles if you decide to use the renderer.

6.1.1 Shading modes

The easiest way to start a render is with the use of your shading modes in the 3D Viewport. If you look to the right of your header, you will see the shading modes (Figure 6.2).

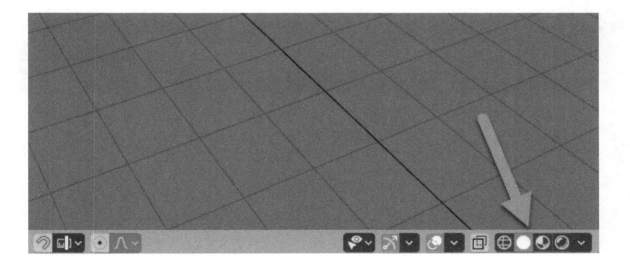

Figure 6.2 - *Shading modes*

With the last button on the right, you will get a rendered view from your scene. If you are using Eevee, you won't notice any slowdowns or performance issues. However, changing the renderer to Cycles will probably slow down your computer and give you a great impression on the differences between Cycles and Eevee.

If you want to have a view if your scene with textures and a rough preview of the lights, you can use the Look Dev mode. The shortcut to quickly change shading modes is the Z key.

For the Viewport shading, you can still choose different lighting modes for the preview and also enable Scene Lights and other options. If you select the Look Dev mode, you will see an HDR map for and allow scene lights to (Figure 6.3).

Figure 6.3 - Look Dev options

In the Solid shading, you have additional options to control transparency and also view colors from the model with a material preview and also random tones (Figure 6.4).

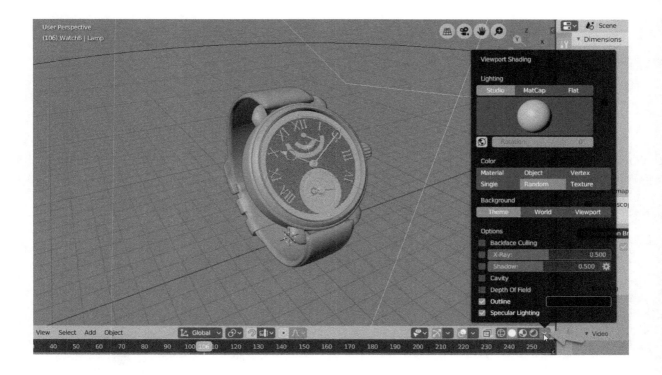

Figure 6.4 - Solid mode options

With the rendered shading mode you have a preview a future render, but it doesn't mean you can't save that image. To save an image from your 3D Viewport, you can use the **View → Viewport Render Image** menu.

6.2 Working with cameras

Before we start rendering images from the scene in Blender, we have to learn how to manage and adjust the camera. The reason for this is because Blender will only render what the active camera is seeing. You can have several cameras in a scene, but only one of them will be active.

The active camera will always show a filled triangle above the icon representing the camera (Figure 6.5).

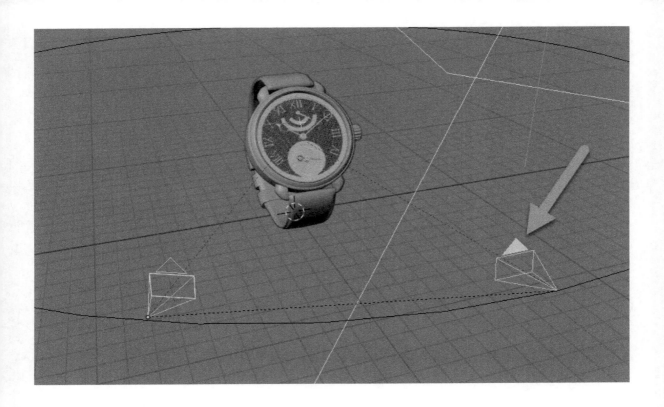

Figure 6.5 - *Active camera*

You can view what the active camera is seeing using the Numpad 0 key. It will make you go to the camera view (Figure 6.6).

Figure 6.6 - *Camera view*

To make another camera active, you can select the camera object and press CTRL+Numpad 0. That will make any selected camera the active one. From the camera view, you can select the camera border and make adjustments to the framing:

– Press the G and R keys to move and rotate the camera

– Press the G key and Z key twice to make a dolly movement

When you press G and the Z key twice, you will start a dolly movement, where you can move the mouse up and down to move your camera forward and backward. That is possible because the local Z-axis from the camera always points towards the same direction it is currently viewing.

By pressing an axis key twice, you will use the local coordinates for a transformation.

Another way to control your framing for the camera is with the focal distance settings. With the camera object selected, you can go for the Object tab, and you will view all options for the camera (Figure 6.7).

175

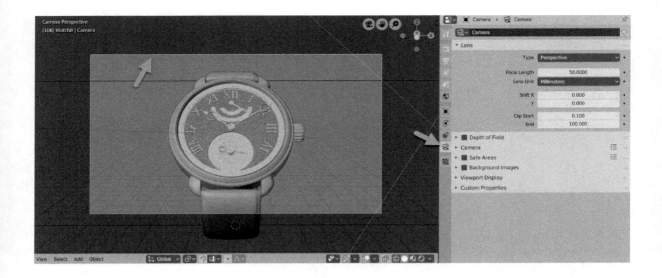

Figure 6.7 - *Camera settings*

At the camera settings, you will find the focal length by the top of your options. With the focal length, we can change the viewing angle our camera have from the scene (Figure 6.8).

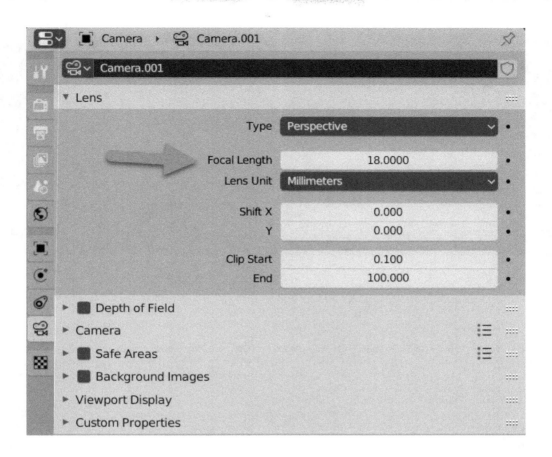

Figure 6.8 - Focal length

Using the millimeters unit, you can get a broad view from the scene with focal distances of 16-20 mm (Figure 6.9).

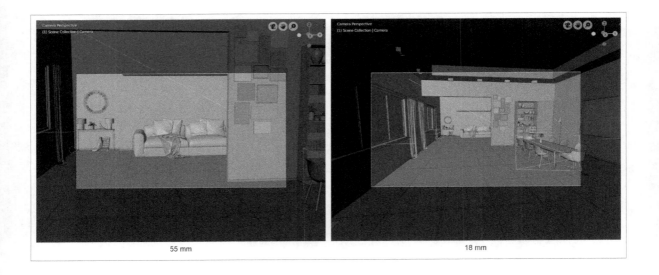

Figure 6.9 - *Focal length difference*

You have to keep in mind that using lower values for the focal distance might give you a more extensive view from the scene but will probably add some distortion to the borders of your render.

6.2.1 Align the camera to view

Using the transformation keys after selecting the camera might help you with an overall framing but will hardly aid with placing the camera for render. The best way to align the camera for rendering is with the use of your 3D Navigation shortcuts.

With the middle mouse button, you can orbit the scene and find a good viewing angle for your render. Once you get the best viewing angle, you can use a shortcut to align your active camera to that view. Press the CTRL+ALT+Numpad 0 keys.

By pressing that keys, you will make your active camera to align with the same viewing angle you have at the moment. It might not still be perfect, but using the transformation keys, you can make the final adjustments to get a perfect framing.

The option is also available from the **View** → **Align View** → **Align Active Camera to View** menu.

6.3 Rendering scenes

Now that you know how to handle the cameras in your scene and control the viewing angle from the active camera, it is time to start rendering the scenes. To render a scene in Blender, you will press the F12 key or use the **Render** → **Render Image** menu.

Once you start a render, you will see the image appearing in the output window. If you are using Eevee, the results will appear in a couple of seconds. In the case of Cycles, it might take a few minutes to appear (Figure 6.10).

Figure 6.10 - *Render results*

The output window will always show the viewing angle from the active camera. If you want to cancel the render at any time, you can always press the ESC key. It may take a while to stop your rendering, especially in Cycles, but it will eventually stop.

6.4 Saving a render

How to save your renders from the Output window in Blender? After you have the render results showing in the Output window will be able to save an image using the Image menu. If you click at the Image menu, you will see an option "Save as…" (Figure 6.11).

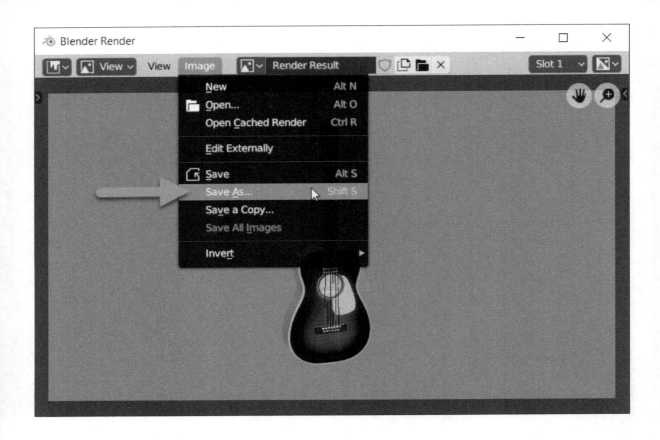

Figure 6.11 - Image menu

From the save options on the left, you will be able to pick a few image formats like:

– PNG

– JPG

– TGA

– TIFF

– EXR

To always keep your render results with the highest possible quality, you should always save your projects as PNG files first. If you need a smaller version later, you can convert the PNG to a JPG file.

The reason to keep your renders as PNG files is that it uses a type of compression for images called lossless. With this method, you will get larger files but not data loss from your renders. A JPG file uses a compression method called lossy, which will exclude some data to reduce file size.

6.4.1 Image settings for rendering

An important setting for any render in Blender is the resolution of your images, which is also a factor that will determine how long it will take for a render to finish. For instance, rendering an image with 300 x 200 pixels will be a lot faster than a 4K image with 4096 x 2160 pixels.

You will find the resolution settings in the Output tab at the Properties Editor (Figure 6.12).

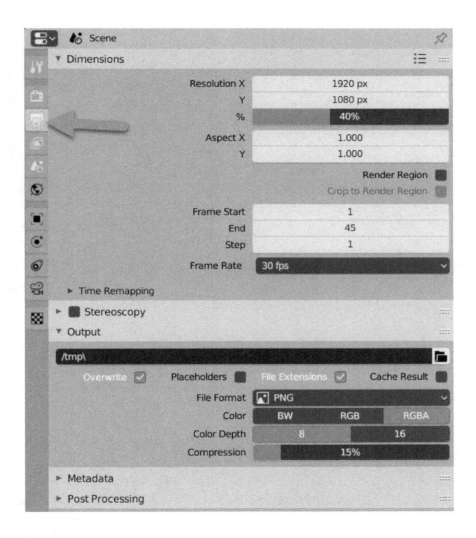

Figure 6.12 - *Output settings*

In the settings, you can manually type the size you wish to use for a render or get a resolution from the presets available right above the manual settings for resolution (Figure 6.13).

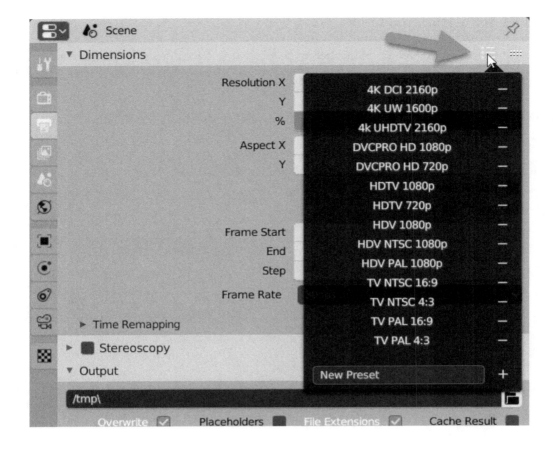

Figure 6.13 - Resolution settings

You can also choose your image format in the Output tab and color settings. One of the benefits of using a PNG file besides the quality is the possibility of using the RGBA color format. By using RGBA, you can have a transparent background for your images (Figure 6.14).

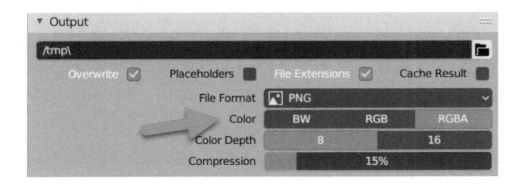

Figure 6.14 - *Color settings*

In the render settings, you can enable at the Film settings an option called "Transparent" and your renders will have a transparent background. The option will work for both Cycles and Eevee (Figure 6.15).

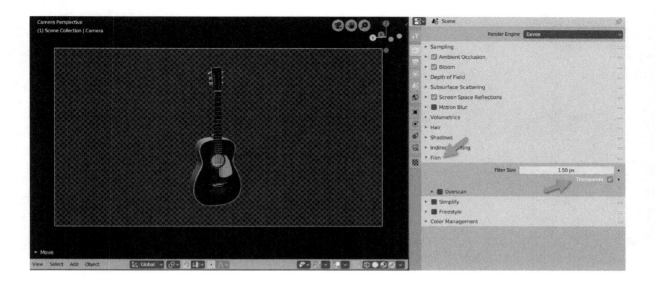

Figure 6.15 - *Transparent option*

Why would you want a transparent background for an image? That will make your work more comfortable if you have to compose the render results with a background or any other image.

The JPG format used by Blender doesn't support transparent backgrounds, which will make you have a color instead of transparent pixels for the background in case you save the render results as a JPG.

6.5 Environmental lights

One of the first steps a lot of artists will take when they start to work on lights for a scene in Blender is to use an environmental light. That is a light coming from the background, which could add a significant amount of light to the scene.

An environmental light will use the background of your scene and also a special type of image called HDR. An HDR image is useful for your environmental lights because:

— They store information about lights for the moment the map got created.

— Since your image will stay in the background, it will reflect on glossy surfaces across the scene.

— It may work as the background for your scene.

For instance, if you get an HDR image for bright sky daylight and add it to the background of your scene, it will generate the same type of lights for the render (Figure 6.16).

Figure 6.16 - *Daylight HDR*

How to use an HDR in your background? You will add an HDR in the World tab at the Properties Editor. There you will find the Surface options. Press the "Use Nodes" button and got o the Color field. Click at the small button on the right of the color selector and pick "Environmental Texture" (Figure 6.17).

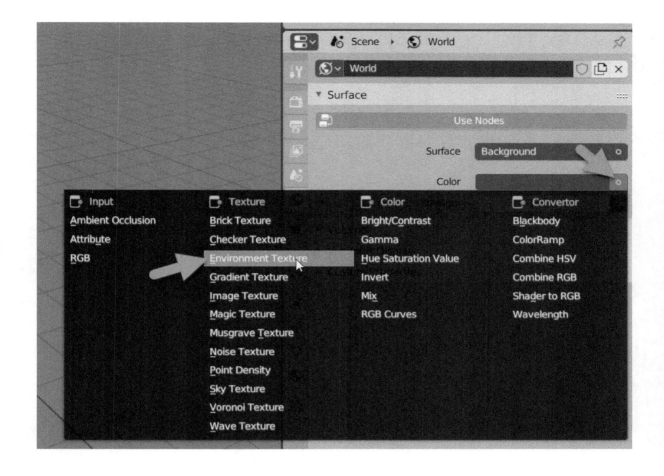

Figure 6.17 - *Environmental Texture*

Once you add the Environmental Texture to the color, you will see options to open a texture file. You can get an HDR map from your computer, and it will appear in the background of your scene if you use the rendered shading mode (Figure 6.18).

HDR in Background

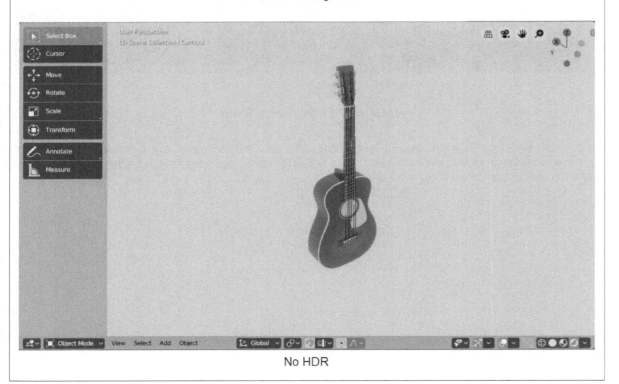

No HDR

Figure 6.18 - HDR in the background

If you don't like the way your HDR map appear in the background, it is possible to control the rotation of your map. Open the Shader Editor and change the View option to World (Figure 6.19).

Figure 6.19 - Shader Editor view

It will make you view the Nodes for the World tab options, and the HDR map will be there for editing. You will add the same Texture Coordinates and Mapping we used from chapter 5 (Figure 6.20).

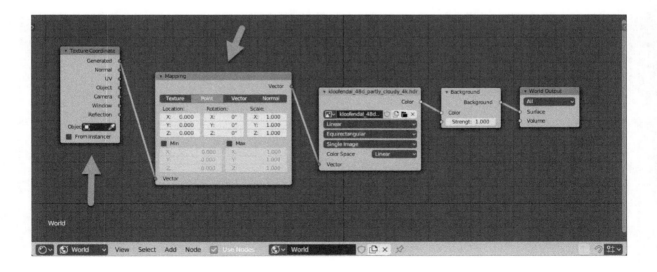

Figure 6.20 - Nodes for rotation

Connect the Texture Coordinates and the Mapping to the Image Texture Node, and you will be able to control the HDR rotation with the Rotation settings from the Mapping Node.

A few points regarding HDR maps for both Cycles and Eevee:

– In Cycles, you will get lights and shadows from HDR maps.

– Eevee can't cast shadows from HDR maps, which makes them less useful for real-time render.

– An HDR map might create different types of lighting. Usually, you can get an idea about the lighting in the preview from the library where you download the HDR map.

You can get dozens of free HDR maps for your projects in hdrhaven.com in public domain. They offer options with multiple types of lights and locations with maps.

Tip: You can download public domain HDR maps from hdrihaven.com for any project in Blender.

6.6 Illumination and types of lights

The environmental lights will be a great help as a starting point for any project, but you will also have to add some light sources to the scene. For instance, if you use Eevee for rendering your scenes, a light source will be the best choice to replace an HDR map since it cant cast shadows in real-time.

In Blender, you can create several types of lights with the SHIFT+A key (Figure 6.21).

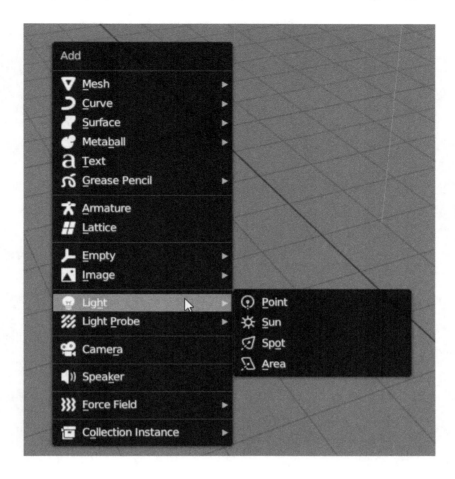

Figure 6.21 - Lights options

The list has options for lights such as:

- **Point**: Emit light from a single point in space in all directions.

- **Sun**: Simulate a distant light source that behaves like the Sun.

- **Spot**: A point that cast light in a cone shape.

- **Area**: A squared shape that emits lights from all the available shape.

Each one of the options for lights will have a purpose in a project. For instance, in a scene that tries to simulate daylight, you will probably use a Sun in combination with an HDR map for a Cycles render.

You can create each one of the lights using the SHIFT+A key or change the type of an existing light source by selecting it and opening the Object Data tab. There you will see buttons at the top where you can quickly change the type of light (Figure 6.22).

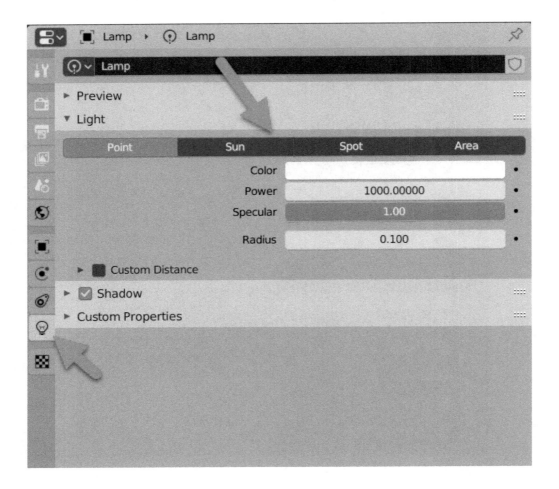

Figure 6.22 - *Light types*

The Object Data tab also holds all options regarding lights where you can control:

– Shadows

– Color

– Power

Besides those settings, you will also find specific options for each one of the lights. For instance, in the Area light options, you will be able to set the size of your area. The Spot will show controls for the cone projection.

The options for each light will change based on the renderer you choose for your project. In Figure 6.23, you can see a comparison between settings for an Area light with Eevee or Cycles.

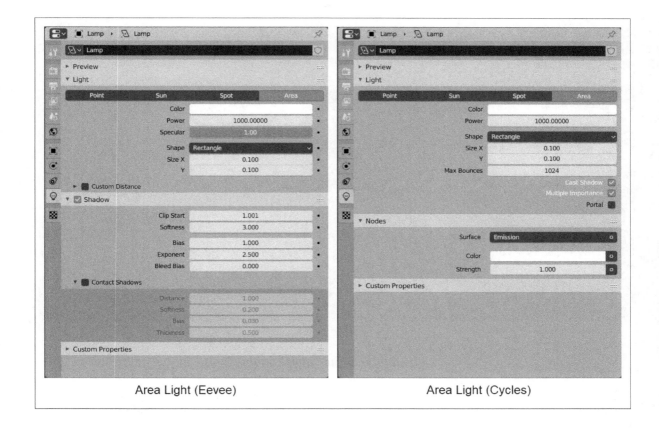

Figure 6.23 - *Comparing light settings*

In the shadow settings, you will see the most significant difference with more options to control shadows when you select Eevee as a renderer.

6.7 Quick setup for rendering

Since each renderer requires specific settings to achieve good lighting results, we will use a simple scene shown in Figure 6.24 to apply a quick setup using both Eevee and Cycles. In the process, we will also change settings for lights and shadows.

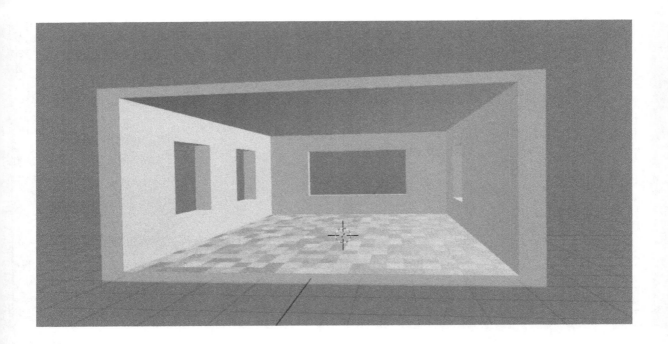

Figure 6.24 - *Scene for quick setup*

From that scene, you will learn how to prepare a project for rendering with both engines. The scenes in Blender and any other software will require specific settings for each type of project, and you will have to make adjustments to achieve good results.

However, using the following quick setup will work as a starting point.

6.7.1 Quick setup for render with Eevee

To render a scene in Eevee, we have to consider a few details regarding the renderer. With Eevee, you will have to take special attention to:

- **Indirect Lights**: Eevee can't generate indirect lights from light sources alone. We have to use probes to calculate indirect bounces.

- **Reflections**: Another feature that you will have to emulate with probes are reflections from glossy surfaces.

- **Environmental lights**: With Eevee, you won't get shadows from HDR maps used in the background of your scene. One of the best choices to replace HDR maps is an Area Light.

- **Light bleed**: A problem that you may encounter in projects rendered with Eevee is light bleed. That might appear due to several factors like 3D models with walls that don't have any thickness or shadows settings.

As a first step for the scene, you should add an Area Light. Using the rotation and move shortcuts, you can place the light in the background of the model, far away from the model. Also, use light settings to increase the size of that light until it became much larger than the model.

In the settings for the light, you should enable the shadows and also contact shadows (Figure 6.25).

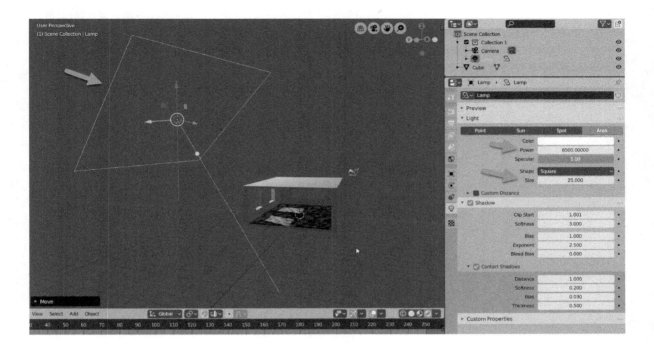

Figure 6.25 - Area as the environmental light

Besides an Area light in the background, you can also add one Area Light to each one of the windows to increase the illumination in the scene. Use the settings from the lights to adjust the size for each Area Light (Figure 6.26).

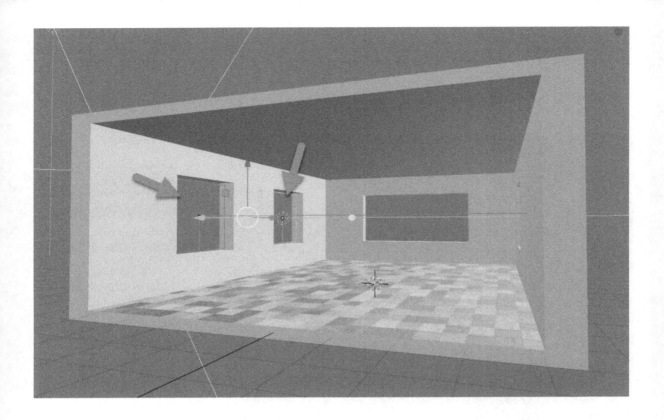

Figure 6.26 - *Area lights in windows*

Since Eevee cant handles indirect lights for rendering, we have to use a probe for that calculations. For indirect lights, you will use an Irradiance Volume. Press the SHIFT+A keys, and from the Light Probes group, add an Irradiance Volume.

Select the Irradiance Volume and using the S key scale it until it covers the entire scene (Figure 6.27).

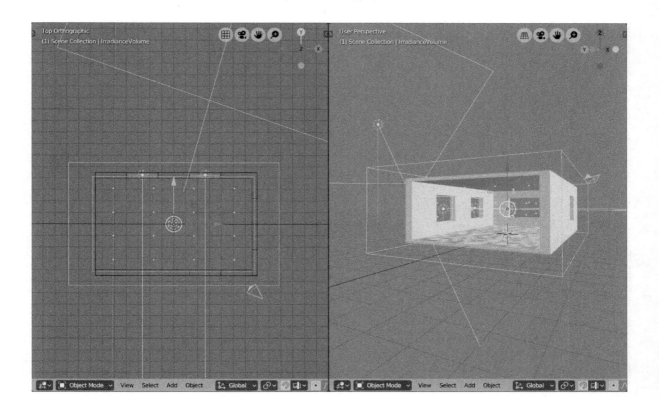

Figure 6.27 - *Irradiance Volume in the scene*

The next probe we will need is a Reflection Cubemap that will capture reflections and cast them in glossy surfaces. Press SHIFT+A again and from the Light Probes group, add a Reflection Cubemap. Using the G key, you can raise the probe from the ground and place it in the middle of your scene.

Use a scale transformation to increase the size of your probe until it becomes bigger than your scene (Figure 6.28).

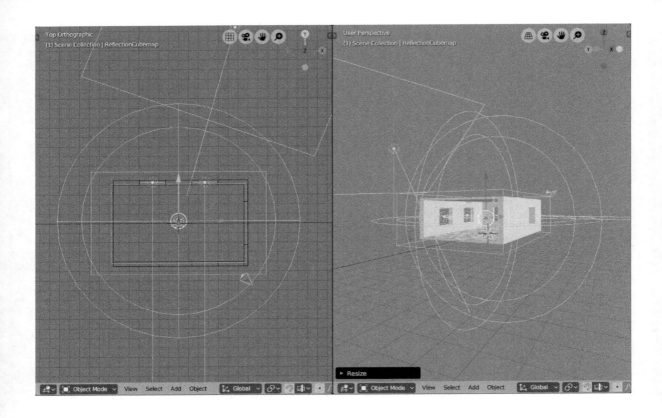

Figure 6.28 - Reflection Cubemap

It is time to use the settings from the Render tab in the Properties Editor. There you will find the Indirect Lighting settings and press the Bake Indirect Lighting button. It will start to calculate indirect lights and reflections for the two probes (Figure 6.29).

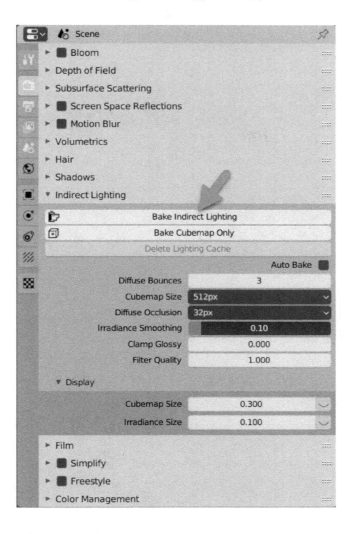

Figure 6.29 - *Indirect lights baking*

You will see the progress at the status bar of your interface. Now, we can make additional enhancements to the scene:

– **Enable Ambient Occlusion**: That will generate contact shadows.

– **Enable Screen Space Reflections**: To create reflections based on a mirror image of your scene.

– **In the Shadows settings enable High Bitdepth and Soft Shadows**: To increase the quality of all shadows.

– **In the Shadow settings change the Cube Size and Cascade Size for 1024px and 2048px respectively**: That will create better borders for all shadows.

Before you render the scene, you can use the rendered shading mode from Eevee to adjust lights even further using the Color Management options (Figure 6.30).

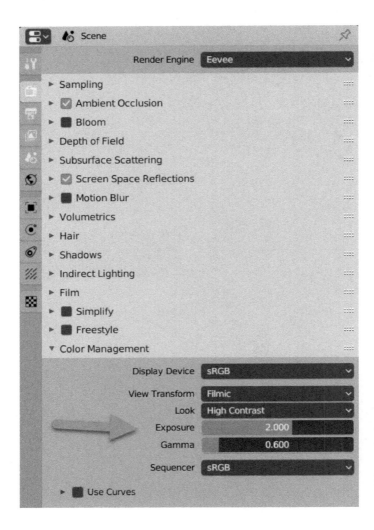

Figure 6.30 - Color Management

With the exposure settings, you can increase the brightness of the scene (Figure 6.31).

Exposure = 1.00

Exposure = 2.00

Figure 6.31 - *Exposure settings*

If you press the F12 key after you enable all those settings, you will get the rendered image from Eevee. The workflow is a basic guide on how to prepare any scene to render in real-time. It may not be the most accurate visualization of a scene regarding realism, but it is fast.

Tip: Use the settings from the Output tab to choose the resolution for your render images.

6.7.2 Quick setup for render with Cycles

Unlike Eevee, you can use a more direct approach with Cycles, and we don't have to use any probe to process indirect lights. However, you will have to wait a little longer for the render to finish.

The first thing you will have to do is change the render engine from Eevee to Cycles because Blender will always start with Eevee as the default renderer.

With Cycles, we can use an HDR map as the environmental light to give an initial boost in the scene illumination. Go to the World tab and add an HDR map to the background (Figure 6.32).

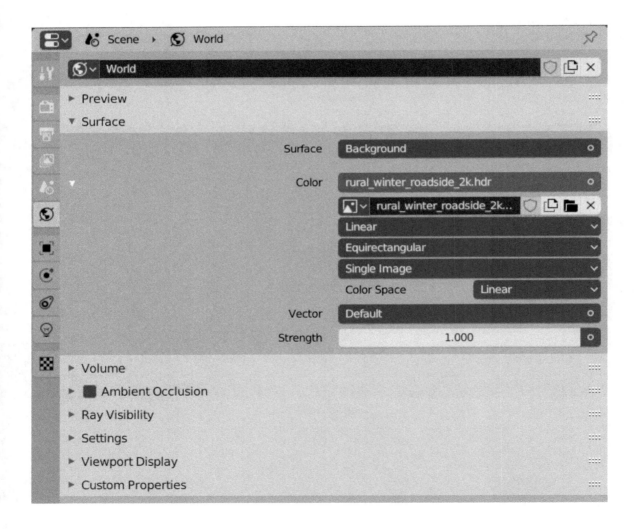

Figure 6.32 - HDR in the background

Adjust the power level of your HDR map in the World tab, and we can move on to the next step.

For a daylight simulation with Cycles, we will use two types of lights. The first one will be a Sunlight that you will place in the location where you wish the Sun will generate lighting and cast shadows. Also, enable shadows in the Sun settings and change the Angle value to a number close to zero like "0.05" to get hard edge shadows (Figure 6.33).

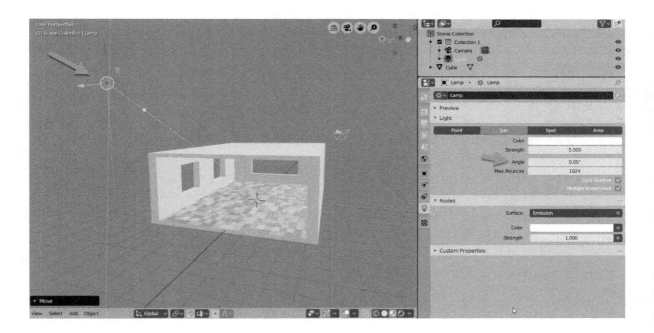

Figure 6.33 - Sun settings

You can use the R key to rotate the Sun and find a good location for the light.

In some cases, using Sunlight alone won't add the necessary energy to the scene. Using Area lights in each window will also help with that type of project. You have to disable the shadow casting for those lights and also scale the lights to make them fit the same size from each window (Figure 6.34).

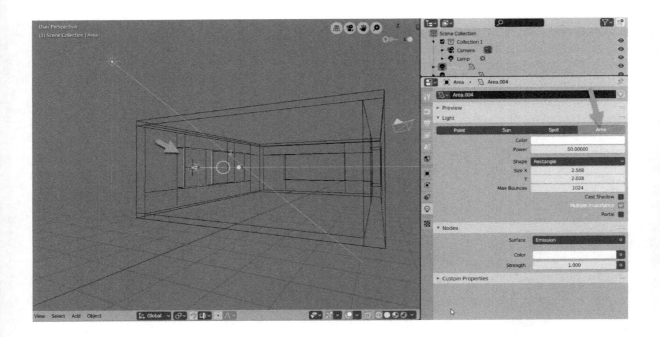

Figure 6.34 - Area light settings

As part of the process of getting lights with the correct settings, you will have to play with the Strength settings for all sources to find the best balance.

If you use the shading mode for Cycles at this point, you will have a great idea of the differences from Eevee. You will get a slow process of rendering, starting with a grainy image that will stop at 32 interactions (Figure 6.35).

Figure 6.35 - *Render preview with Cycles*

Those interactions in Cycles have a limit that you will set at the Render tab.

Tip: *You can interrupt the render for your preview using the pause button next to the shading modes selector.*

In the Sampling field, you will find the limit for interactions in the render and previews. The default value for your 3D Viewport will always start with 32 (Figure 6.36).

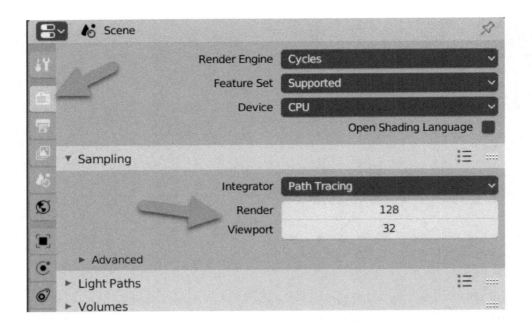

Figure 6.36 - Render settings

One of the biggest challenges to render a scene in Cycles is to find an optimal sample value that will give you a noiseless image. Usually, a value between 500 and 1000 will give you good results, but it will depend on several factors. The difference in render times from 500 to 1000 samples could be a few hours.

To help you using fewer samples and getting clean images, we can enable the Denoiser tool in Cycles. Go to the View Layer tab and enable the Denoiser tool (Figure 6.37).

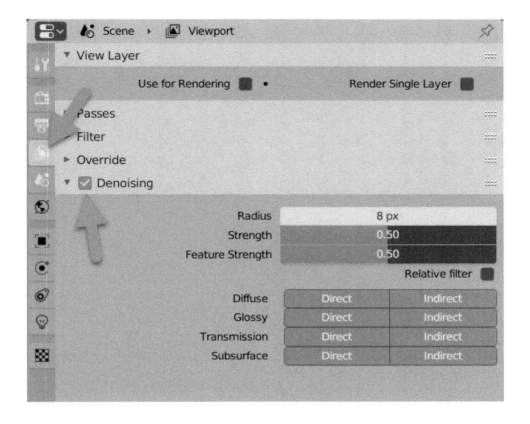

Figure 6.37 - *Denoiser tool*

That will give you room to use fewer samples and still get a clean image. Even with the Denoiser, you will have to perform a few tests to find what is the optimal sample value for your project.

In our case, a sample count of 500 with the Denoiser will give good results. Adjust the camera and start your render. Since we are using Cycles, you will have to wait a couple of minutes. The Denoiser only works in the Render process and won't take any effect in the preview at the 3D Viewport.

You must press F12 to render if you want to see the Denoiser in action.

The total render time for this particular render was 12 minutes, using the GPU to speed up the process. You can select the GPU for rendering in the Render tab (Figure 6.38).

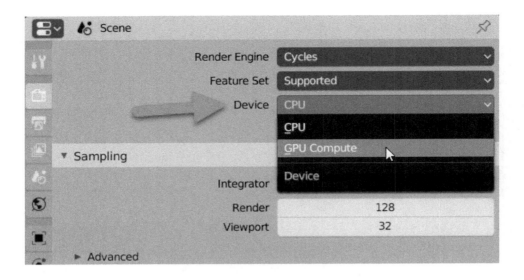

Figure 6.38 - *Choosing the GPU*

If you have a computer with a dedicated GPU, you should try to render using the device for better performance with Cycles. After you render the scene, it is time to make adjustments to the brightness of your scene with the Color Management options (Figure 6.39).

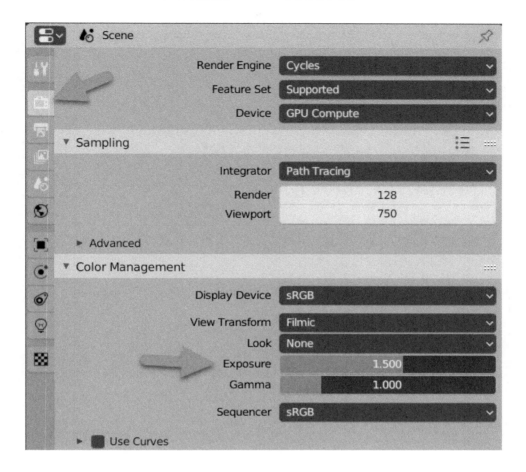

Figure 6.39 - *Color management*

Use the exposure settings to get a brighter result for the image. You can use the color management options after the render process, which will save you an incredible amount of time (Figure 6.40).

Exposure = 0.00

Exposure = 1.50

Figure 6.40 - *Exposure settings*

Save the render results to disk, and you will have a full render in Cycles.

What is next?

Unlike many aspects of projects related to 3D modeling where you will repeat steps and tool to build a complex object, you will have to adapt the lights in both Eevee and Cycles for all new projects.

That is because each project will feature unique features for scale, materials, and context. For that reason, you will have to find the best settings for each new scene. With practice, you will learn that most scenes share some standard settings like using an environment map.

But for lights setup, you will have to make adjusted in each scene.

The best way to develop your skills for lighting is by observing an image like a photo an trying to reproduce the effect and shading with the options in Blender.

Following our learning about how to render still images in this chapter, you will find how to create videos and sequences of images from animations. Blender is a powerful software to create animations, and you will learn how to add keyframes to develop all kinds of motion.

Chapter 7 - Animation and motion with Blender

When you render a single image in Blender for any project, you are handling an animation frame even without any motion. One of the primary purposes of Blender is to create animations, and it has lots of features and tools for that task.

In this chapter, you will learn how to create animation with the use of something called keyframe. The keyframes allow us to mark a certain property in time. When you have multiple keyframes with different values, you will create animations.

Here is a list of what you will learn in this chapter:

- How animations work in Blender

- Controlling and managing frames and length for animations

- Choosing the FPS for animations

- Add/Remove and manage keyframes

- Creating simple animations with keyframes

- Adjusting animation timing

- Making linear animations using curves

7.1 How to make an animation with Blender?

The technique Blender uses to create animations has a name of interpolation, which will work bases on a combination of keyframes and transformations along a timeline. Each keyframe will define a property of an object at a certain point in time.

If you have enough keyframes in a timeline, you will end up with animation. A timeline for animations uses frames to identify the time. Usually, you will get 24 to 30 frames for one second of animation. For instance, an animation that has 5 seconds with 30 frames per second will use a total of 150 frames.

The value of frames per second has a name of frame rate, and you will find it in lots of places identified by the acronym FPS. For the rest of the book, we will use FPS to determine the frame rate.

By default in Blender, you will always start with an FPS of 24, which you can change at the Output tab (Figure 7.1).

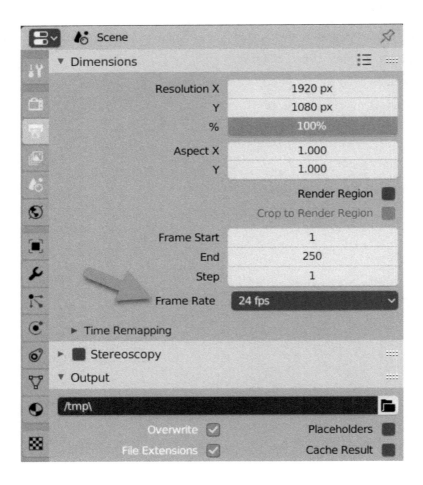

Figure 7.1 - *Frame rate settings*

For video and animation, you will find that most people use 24 or 30 FPS. Since animations can also consume a significant amount of resources, Blender will also limit the total length of animation with a start and end frames. Above the frame rate settings, you can set up the start and end frames (Figure 7.2).

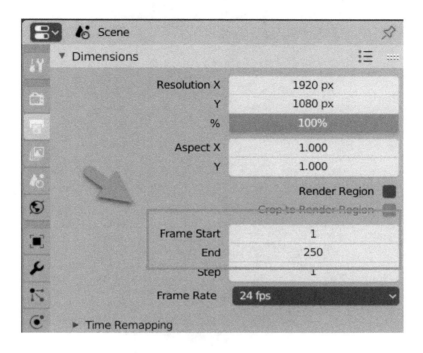

Figure 7.2 - *Start and end frames*

Those values will always begin with 1 and 250 for the start and end, respectively. If you have to create an animation with 3 seconds using a 30 FPS, which will require 90 frames, you can change the start and end to 1 and 90.

If you don't change the start and end, you will still be able to create animations. But your previews for animations will playback not only your 90 frames but all the length until it reaches 250.

7.1.1 Adding keyframes to objects

To add keyframes to any objects in Blender, we can use several methods from a simple shortcut key or with a right-click. No matter the way you choose to create keyframes, you won't be able to make animations without them. After you select an object, you can use the I key to add a keyframe.

Once you press the I key, you will see a list with all available keyframe types (Figure 7.3).

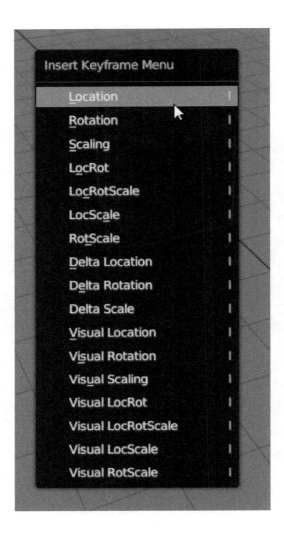

Figure 7.3 - Keyframe types

You must choose the keyframe type for an animation based on the kind of motion you want to create. The keyframe type has a direct relation to the property you are animating.

For instance, if you are trying to animate a rotation, you will create a keyframe using the Rotation type. In case you want to make a rotation and scale animation at the same time, you can use the RotScale keyframe type.

The keyframe type selection will only appear when you are creating keyframes in the 3D Viewport. Another way to insert keyframes to objects is with a right-click on the 3D Viewport. At the Context menu, you will choose the "Insert keyframe..." option (Figure 7.4).

Figure 7.4 - *Context menu*

By the way, you will create keyframes in Object Mode for animation.

There are other methods to create keyframes in the Sidebar or using the Properties Editor and the Object tab. If you right-click at any numeric property like a location, you will see two options (Figure 7.5).

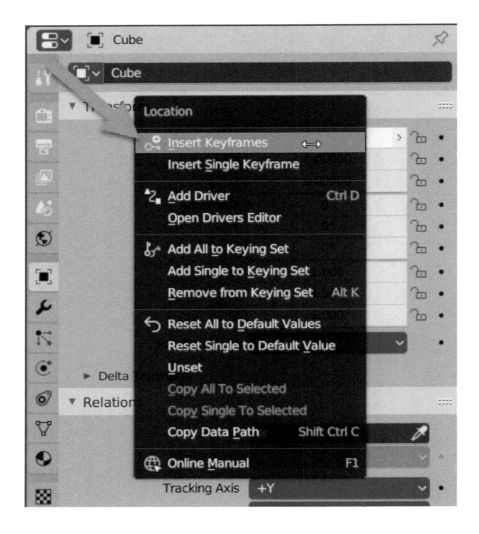

Figure 7.5 - Inserting keyframes in properties

For instance, if you right-click at the X location field, you will see two options:

- **Insert keyframes**: Creates a keyframe for all three axes in the location property.
- **Insert Single Keyframe**: Adds a keyframe only to the X location property.

By using the right-click at any property, you won't have to make any selection for keyframe types, because you are already interacting with a single property. You will have to choose whether you will add the keyframe to a single axis or all three of them. That will depend on the type of animation you want to create.

After you add the keyframe to those properties, you will see a yellow background for the field with a keyframe. On the right, you will also notice that a diamond-shaped symbol will appear on top of the small dot available in all properties (Figure 7.6).

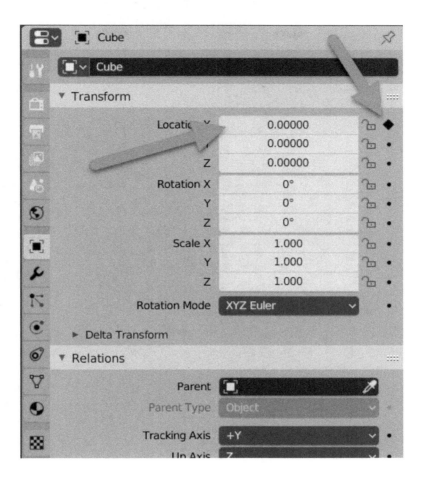

Figure 7.6 - Keyframe in property

Another way to add keyframes to any object is by click at those dots, which will make the diamond shape icon appear. It identifies a keyframe for that property.

Info: *The interpolation process uses the keyframes to create animation. It takes the difference in properties between two keyframes and creates all intermediate values automatically.*

7.1.2 Removing and updating keyframes

What if you want to remove a keyframe? You can easily remove and manage keyframes with a right-click at the property value that has a keyframe. If you right-click at in a property that has keyframes, you will see several options to manage keyframes (Figure 7.7).

217

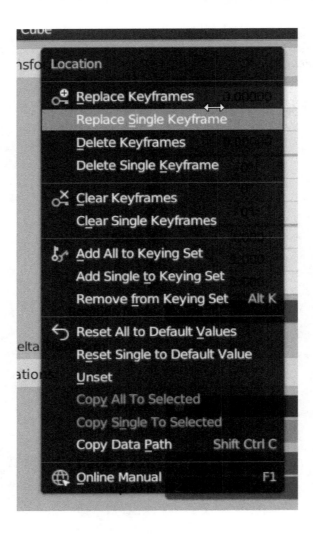

Figure 7.7 - Managing keyframes

There is more than one option to manage keyframes:

- **Replace keyframes**: Updates the property value of all keyframes in the property and keep them in the same locations in time.

- **Replace Single Keyframe**: Changes the value of your selected keyframe for that particular moment in time.

- **Delete Keyframes**: Removes all keyframes from the object for that specific property in a single frame.

- **Delete Single Keyframe**: Excludes only the selected keyframe for that frame.

- **Clear Keyframes**: Removes all keyframes in all properties for the entire timeline.

– **Clear Single keyframes**: Removes all keyframes for the property selected in all timeline.

Notice that you can use either the Delete or Clear keyframes to remove animation data from an object. The difference between them is that you will be able to remove the keyframes for a single frame or the entire animation.

7.1.3 Timeline navigation

An essential tool for your animation production in Blender is the ability to navigate in the timeline. You will have a delimited set of frames to navigate and choosing the right frame to insert a keyframe is critical for the process.

In the 3D Viewport, you will find that it displays the current frame from your animation on the left of your active collection. Using the Timeline Editor, you will also be able to see the current frame and also choose the start and end frames (Figure 7.8).

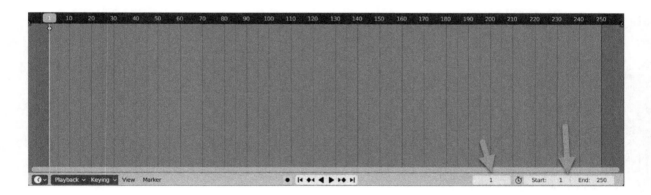

Figure 7.8 - *Timeline Editor*

A few shortcuts you will want to use for animation control:

– **SPACEBAR**: Play the animation.

– **LEFT ARROW**: Jump one frame backward.

– **RIGHT ARROW**: Jump one frame forward.

– **UP ARROW**: Jump to the next keyframe.

– **DOWN ARROW**: Jump to the previous keyframe.

– **SHIFT+LEFT ARROW**: Jump to the start frame.

– **SHIFT+RIGHT ARROW**: Jump to the end frame.

You can also navigate in the Timeline using the playback head, which is the vertical green line marking the current frame. Using the left mouse button, you can click and drag your line to change the current frame.

That same line also appears in several other editors that handle animation data in Blender, like the Graph Editor and the Dopesheet.

7.2 Creating a simple animation

Now that we know how to create keyframes and navigate using the Timeline Editor, it is time to make a simple animation. The purpose of the animation is making an object move in the 3D Viewport. You can use any object as an example for the animation.

In our case, we can grab a text object that you can create using the SHIFT+A keys and choosing the Text option. To edit the text contents, you can go to Edit Mode and replace the text.

The animation will use the following data:

- **Length**: 2 seconds
- **FPS**: 30
- **Start frame**: 1
- **End frame**: 60

You can change most of the settings for this animation in the Timeline Editor. Only the FPS will require you to use the Output tab to change from 24 to 30 the frame rate.

Tip: You can press the Home key to adjust the zoom of your Timeline editor after you set the Start and End frames.

Our object will start on the left side of our 3D Viewport and move to the right side. The animation will use location keyframes. Select the object you want to animate and make sure frame 1 is your current frame (Figure 7.9).

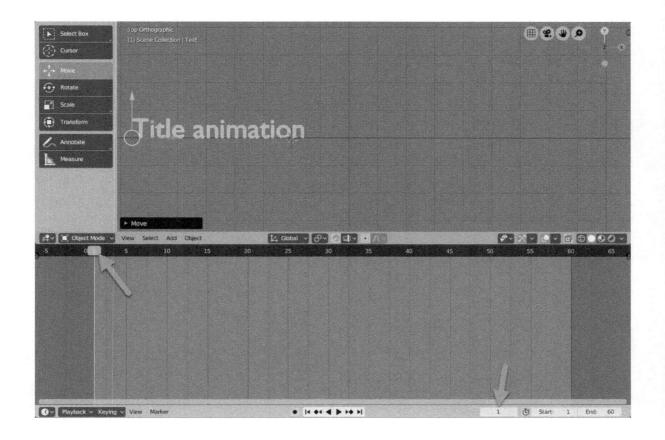

Figure 7.9 - Animation start

Press the I key and choose a location keyframe. You can also use the Sidebar or the Object tab in the Properties Editor. There you will right-click above the Location field and choose Insert Keyframes.

You will see that your Timeline now displays a diamond-shaped icon for the selected object in frame 1 (Figure 7.10). The object name and active collection will also turn to yellow.

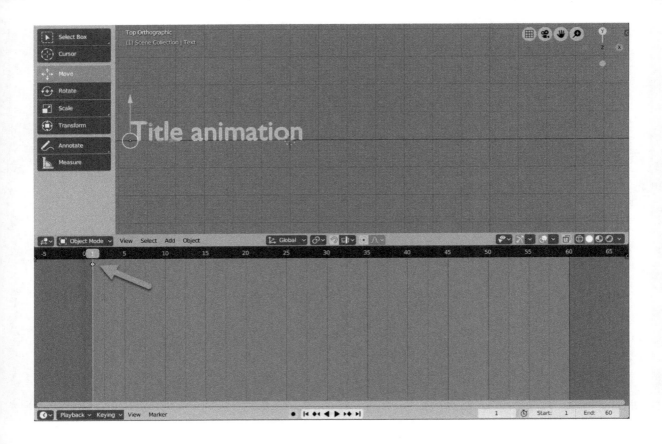

Figure 7.10 - Timeline with keyframe

Move the current frame to 60 and keep the object selected. Press the G key and move the object to the right side of your 3D Viewport once the object is in the right side press the I key and choose location. A new keyframe will appear in the Timeline (Figure 7.11).

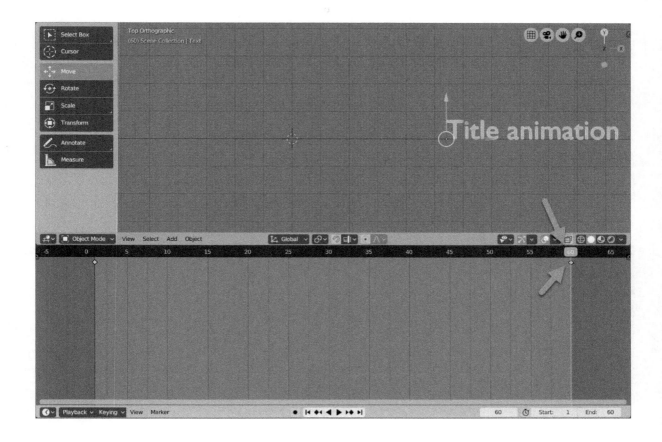

Figure 7.11 - Second keyframe

If you press the SPACEBAR or the play button in the Timeline, you will see an animation from the object moving from left to right.

We can expand the animation, making the object stay still for one second and then go back to the left side of your screen. First, we will have to add two seconds to the total length of our animation. In the Timeline Editor change the End frame from 60 to 120.

Tip: Use the mouse wheel to adjust the zoom and view all frames from 1 to 120.

To make your object stay still in animation you will repeat the same keyframe. In our case, you can set the current frame to 90 and press the I key with the object selected. Choose the location keyframe type.

You will notice that from frames 60 to 90, you will have a solid line connecting both keyframes in the Timeline (Figure 7.12).

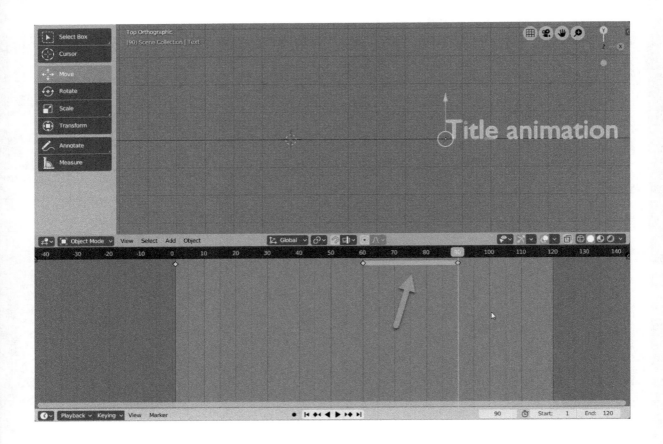

Figure 7.12 - *Timeline with solid lines*

That is a visual representation of two keyframes with no changes between two keyframes. Since we didn't move the object, it has the same value for both keyframes.

Go to frame 120 and move your object to the left side of your screen. Once there, you can press the I key and choose the location type. Press the SPACEBAR, and you will see the object starting in the left and moving to the right. After staying still for one second, it will go back to the left side.

Besides the solid line connecting two keyframes that shares the same data in the Timeline, you will also find another visual code. It shows that a property has animation in the Sidebar and Object tab (Figure 7.13).

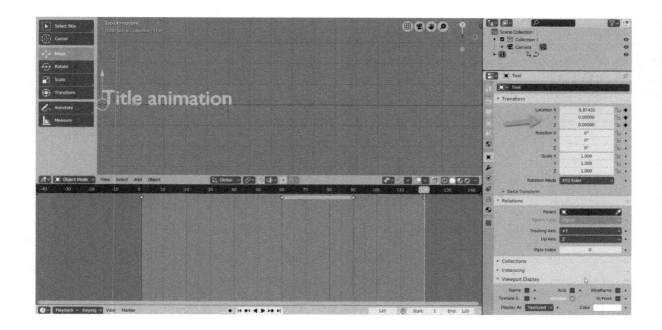

Figure 7.13 - *Color codes*

When you are in a frame where the selected object has a keyframe, your property will display a yellow background. For the intermediate frames where interpolation is occurring the property background will be green.

7.3 Managing animation timing

After you create an animation in Blender, you might want to make changes to the timing and speed of your animation. To make such adjustments, you will have to move the keyframes for timing adjustments.

For instance, if you take the animation, we created in section 7.2 for timing adjustments, we can do that straight in the Timeline Editor. There you can select each keyframe, and with the G key move them forward or backward.

When you make two keyframes closer to each other, you will make the animation go faster. If you increase the distance between them, you will get a slower movement (Figure 7.14).

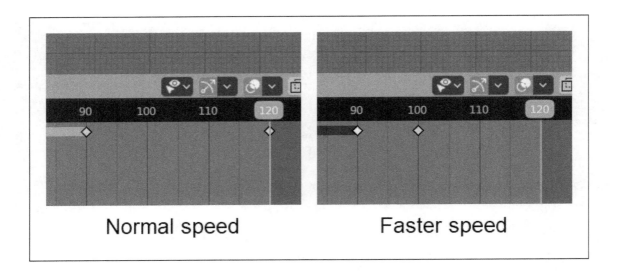

Figure 7.14 - *Timing adjustments for keyframes*

To manipulate keyframes in the Timeline or any other editor in Blender, you will use the same selection keys and transformations used in 3D modeling.

If you want to adjust the entire animation timing, a scale transformation will help. Press the A key to select all keyframes and use the S key to scale up or down animation as the whole (Figure 7.15).

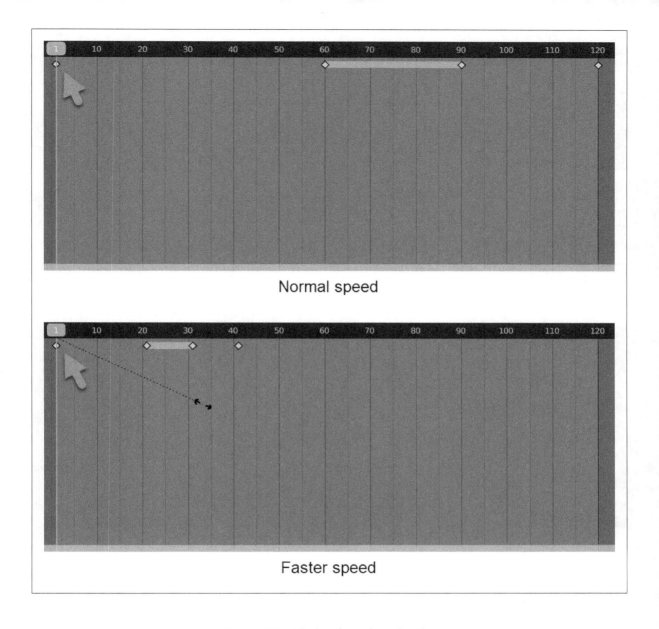

Figure 7.15 - *Timing the entire animation*

By using a scale transformation, you have to be careful with the current frame. That frame will work as the pivot point for the scale. To keep your animation starting in the same frame, make sure you set the current frame at the beginning of your animation.

Using any other frame as the current frame during a scale might completely change the start and end frames of your animation.

Tip: You can also use the Snap at the Timeline Editor. Select a keyframe and press SHIFT+S to show options related to animation.

7.4 Controlling animation with curves

If you take a close look at the animation created in section 7.2, you will notice that it's not a linear motion. The object will gain speed in the beginning and will slow down by the end of each motion in animation that has a name of easing.

Any keyframes you add in Blender will use easing for motion regardless of the property you are trying to animate. To view and edit that type of animation data, we can use the Graph Editor in Blender, which will give as a visual representation of all motion as curves (Figure 7.16).

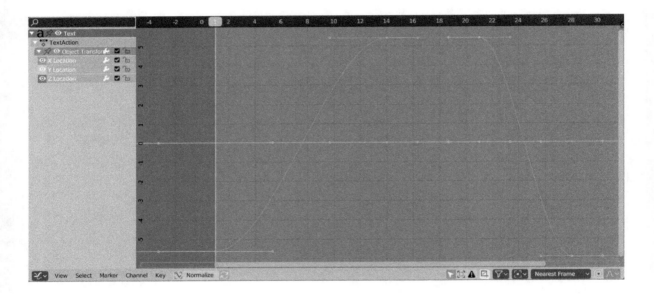

Figure 7.16 - Graph Editor

You can use the same space from the Timeline in the interface to open a Graph Editor. There you will see a to more information than the Timeline. For instance, you will be able to see individual animation channels on the left. Also, some controls to lock animations (padlock icon) and hide curves from the editor (checkbox icon).

The graph will display animation data using the X-axis for the frames and Y-axis for the property value.

You can use the same zoom controls to adjust the viewing of your curves. With the Home key, you can fit all curves and keyframes in the current editor. The keyframes will show up there as small dots (Figure 7.17).

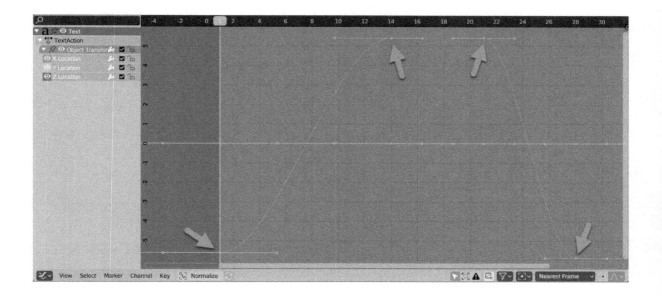

Figure 7.17 - Keyframes in the Graph Editor

If you select a keyframe and use the G key to move it around, you will see the curve structure. Besides the keyframe, you will also see the control handlers (Figure 7.18).

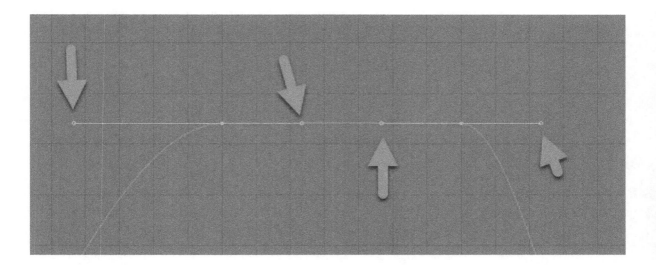

Figure 7.18 - Control handlers

By selecting the handlers, you can deform the curve and change the speed and easing of an animation. With a keyframe selected you can press the N key to open the Sidebar for the Graph Editor and change the values for that particular keyframe (Figure 7.19).

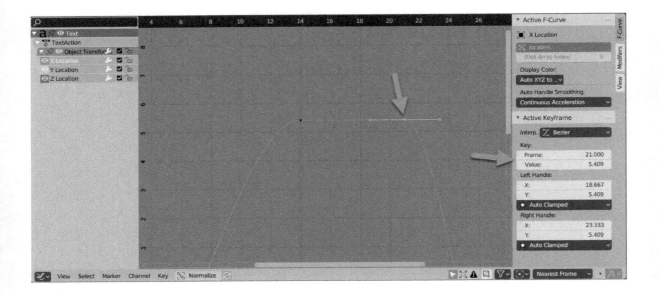

Figure 7.19 - *Keyframe values*

At the Key field, you can change the frame of your keyframe and also the value for the property. That is an easy way to make changes to any keyframe without the need to update any other information.

To remove any easing from the animation, you can change the Interpolation Modes. Press the A key to select all keyframes and in the Graph Editor go to the **Key → Interpolation Mode** menu and choose linear.

That will change your curves to straight lines, which will turn the motion to a linear speed (Figure 7.20).

Interpolation: Bezier   Interpolation: Linear

Figure 7.20 - *Linear motion*

Regarding animation, you will use easing when you want to create natural movement, and for artificial motion, like machines and scripts, you can use the Linear interpolation.

7.5 Hierarchies for animations

For animation projects that demand multiple objects to interact with each other too will want to create hierarchies to make complex animations. When you make those hierarchies, it will be possible to control motion using parent objects.

In Blender, you will create hierarchies for animation using the CTRL+P keys to make a parent. To make it easier to understand, we can name two objects in a hierarchy as parent and child:

- **Parent**: Object that can receive transformations and will replicate all of them to the children.
- **Child**: Object that receives all effects from the parent. If you rotate or move the parent, all children will also receive the same animation. However, any transformation applied to the child won't affect the parent.

For instance, if we have a 3D model like the one shown in Figure 7.21, we can make it work as a robotic arm. All we have to do is adjust the correct parenting between each object.

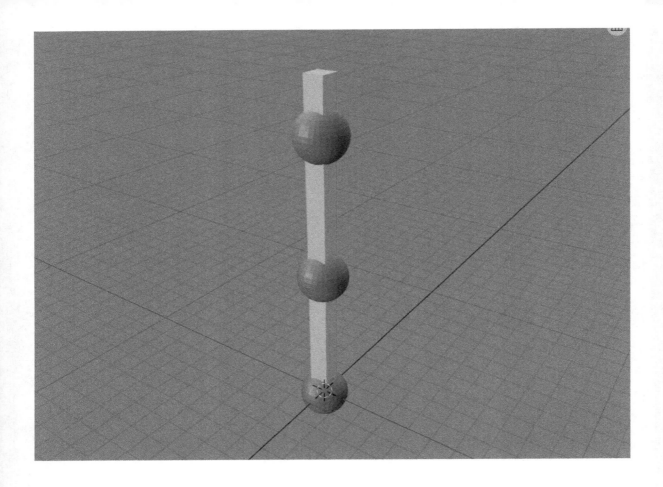

Figure 7.21 - *Objects for robotic arm*

For a robotic arm motion, you will use the object near the base as the parent of the structure. Starting with the top two objects, we can first select the child and holding the SHIFT key select the parent (Figure 7.22).

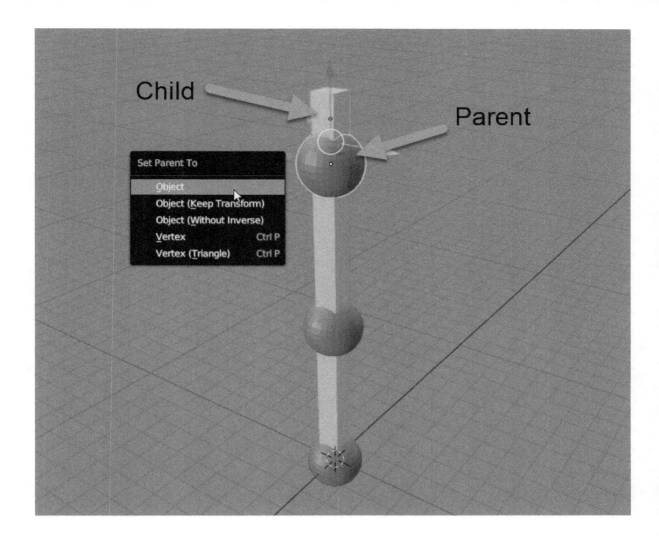

Figure 7.22 - Parenting selection

Press the CTRL+P keys to create a parent and child relation. If you make a mistake, you can press ALT+P to break the connection. How to verify the parenting? Simple, you can select the parent and apply a rotation. You will see the child rotation together with the parent if everything is correct.

Repeat the parenting process for all the other parts of the model according to what Figure 7.23 shows.

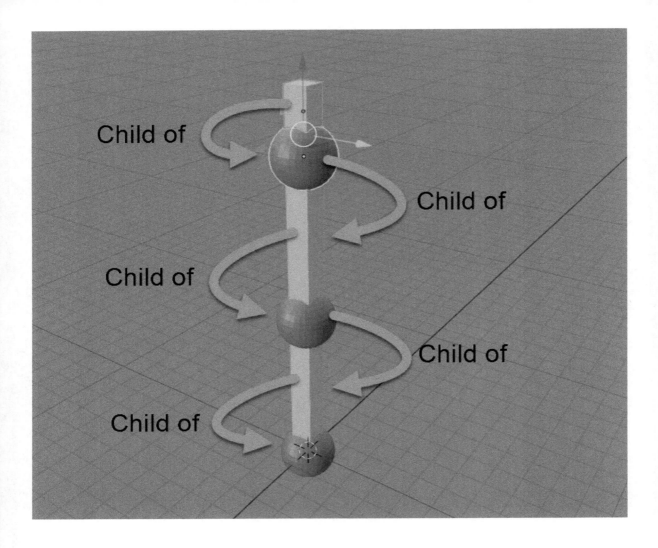

Figure 7.23 - Parenting structure

After you have the full model with parent relations, an animation of the arm will become a lot easier. By selecting the base sphere of the object, you will be able to move and rotate the entire arm. Select the spheres and apply individual rotations to create poses for the arm (Figure 7.24).

Figure 7.24 - Arm positioning

You can apply rotation keyframes to the spheres and make an animation with the arm. In those types of animations, you easily go back to the rest position by clearing the rotation. You can press ALT+R to clear a rotation.

Use the ALT key with any transformation key to return the object property to the original value.

Tip: You can also create an object like the one shown in Figure 7.21 using only cubes and spheres. Apply transformations and move them to stay with the same formation from the image.

7.6 Constraints for animations

In animation projects, you might want to use a special type of tool that will help to create motion with complex relations between objects. With the constraints, we can add rules to the animation and apply keyframes to make objects interact with each other.

You will find in the Properties Editor all options related to constraints in the Object Constraint tab (Figure 7.25).

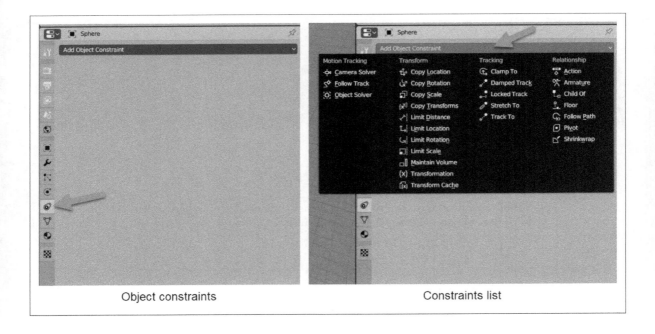

Figure 7.25 - Object constraint

After you apply a constraint to an object, you will have unique options for each one of the tools. In the list you will find:

- **Copy Location, Copy Rotation, and Copy Scale**: Makes the selected object uses the same transformation data from the target object.

- **Limit Location, Limit Rotation, and Limit Scale**: Makes the object chosen receive a limit for each transformation based on a target object.

- **Child of**: You can create parenting relations that can receive keyframes.

You can stack constraints like modifiers and also apply keyframes to the Influence. That opens a world of possible animations we can create using constraints.

7.6.1 Making an arm grab an object

An easy example of what we can do with constraints for animation is to make an arm grab an object. To make our example simple, we can use the same arm created in section 7.5 with the same parenting.

For the animation, we will use the arm, a sphere, and three empties that will help us with the positioning (Figure 7.26).

236

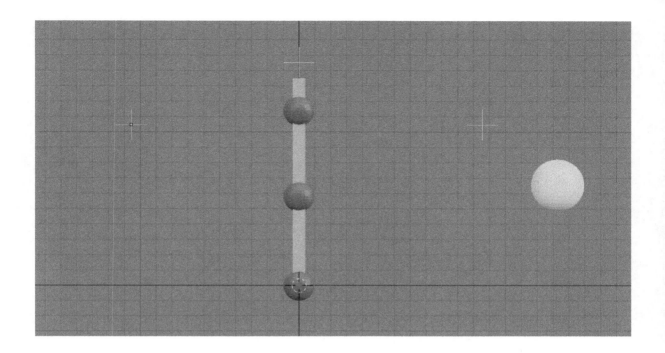

Figure 7.26 - *Scene for animation*

The objective is to make our arm grab the sphere from the left side of the screen, and release it on the right side. It is a simple animation, which would be difficult to create without constraints.

Before we start making the animation, we have to prepare all objects relations. The empty close to the tip of our arm must be a child of the arm "hand." Select the empty first and then the "hand." Press CTRL+P to create parenting.

Info: You will see a dashed line connecting the Empty and "hand" once they have a parenting relation.

Using the F2 key rename the empties with the following names:

− **Empty near the sphere**: firstEmpty

− **Empty near the "hand"**: armEmpty

− **Empty on the right**: endEmpty

Our animation will have 120 frames and an FPS of 30. Using the transformation keys, you can use rotation only transformations to make all moves to the arm:

− **From frame 1 to 30**: Rotate the arm close to the "firstEmpty."

− **From frame 31 to 90**: Rotate the arm to the other side, close to the "endEmpty."

— **From frame 91 to 120**: Rotate the arm away from the "endEmpty."

The animation will happen only in the sphere objects, and to clear your motion between frames 90 and 120, you can press ALT+R.

If you press the SPACEBAR, you will see the arm moving in the 3D Viewport, but the sphere will remain in the same location.

Now, select the sphere object and apply three "Copy Location" constraints. In each constraint, you should choose the target object one of the empties. Change the influence of the constraints with the "endEmpty" and "armEmpty" to zero (Figure 7.27).

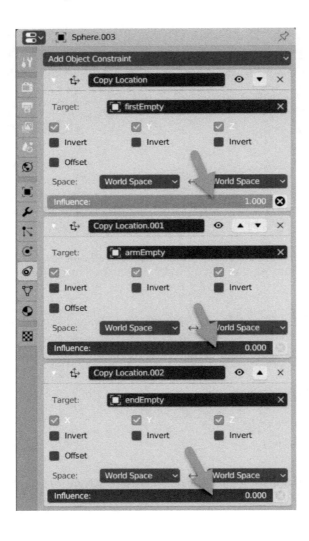

Figure 7.27 - Constraints for sphere

Make sure your current frame is one and apply a keyframe to all influences. You can either right-click on each property and choose "Insert keyframe…" or place the mouse cursor above the influence and press the I key (Figure 7.28).

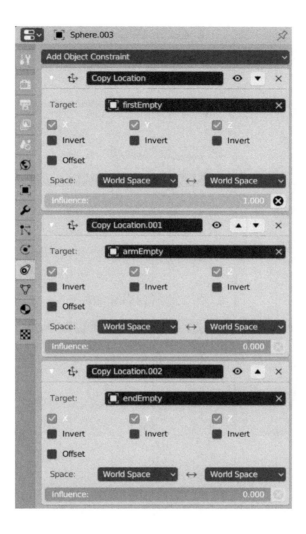

Figure 7.28 - Keyframes for constraints

By the way, you can add keyframes to all properties in Blender using the same procedure.

Got o frame 30 and insert keyframes to all of the influences again. In frame 31, which is the time your arm will get close to the sphere, you will change the influences. Set the influence of the constraint with the "firstEmpty" to zero and the one with "armEmpty" to one (Figure 7.29).

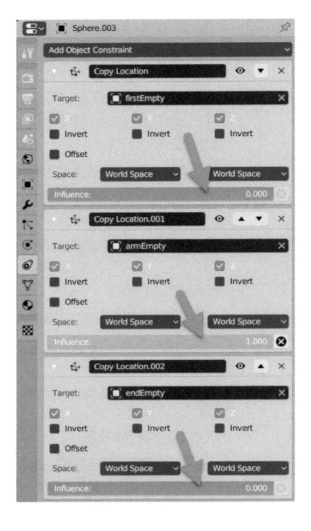

Figure 7.29 - Influences for constraints

Apply keyframes to all constraint influences again. If you preview your animation, you will see that the arm will "grab" the sphere in frame 31. From that point forward, the sphere will follow any movement of the arm.

Go to frame 90 and apply keyframes to all influences in the three constraints. In frame 91, change the influence of the constraint with the "armEmpty" to zero and the "endEmpty" to one. Apply keyframes to all of the constraint influences (Figure 7.30).

Figure 7.30 - *Last keyframes*

If you preview your animation at this moment, you will see the arm moving until it grabs the sphere at frame 31. In the end, it will release the object on the left side of your 3D Viewport, at frame 91.

That is just one example of what we can do with constraints for animations.

What is next?

The creation of animations is a time-consuming task in any software, and you will find that Blender shares that same aspect of animation production. For each idea or project, you have to create animations; it will be necessary sometime, and patients get a quality animation.

A great way to learn and develop skills for animations is to make quick and small projects related to motion graphics. It can be a simple plane with a texture with a logo, which will enter the screen with additional text.

Or you can make fly through animations using only camera motion. Regardless of the project type, you should try to create a small portfolio of animations to develop your skills.

The next chapter will help you with additional information regarding animation production like editing content, adding titles, and making objects follow predefined paths.

Chapter 8 - Animation rendering and composition

In the last chapter of our book, you will improve the tools and options regarding animation production. We will add a missing feature from the Blender camera that lost of artists love to use, which is a target.

By using a particular type of constraint and an Empty, you can create a target that your camera will always follow. You can make obj sets moving around the scene, and your camera will always keep the focus on them.

With the constraint and an option related to curves, we can create another type of animation called "Turntable." In those animations, your objects will stay still, and the camera will "fly" in a circle around the object — a great option to show 3D models in motion.

Here is a list of what you will learn in this chapter:

- How to make a camera always look to the same object with a Track To constraint

- Make objects follow a path in animation

- Creating animation loops in the Graph Editor

- Render and export video for animation

- Use the Video Sequencer Editor

- Edit, Cut, and compose animations with the Sequencer

- Add backgrounds for animations in the Sequencer

- Add titles for animations using the Sequencer

8.1 Following an object with the camera

The camera framing is an important aspect of any project in Blender for both still images and also animations. In animations, you will want to use a feature that will allow the camera to follow an object animation. That will be useful on several occasions where you have an important subject in animation.

To make your camera follow any object in the scene, you will use a constraint called Track To. Since that constraint is important for animations, you can add it to an object in two different ways:

– **Using the Constraint tab at the Properties editor**: Select the camera and add the Track To option.
– **Go to the Object → Track → Track To Constraint menu**: Select the target object first and the camera last. Use the menu option to add the Constraint.

Both options will generate a constraint that you can edit and change options (Figure 8.1).

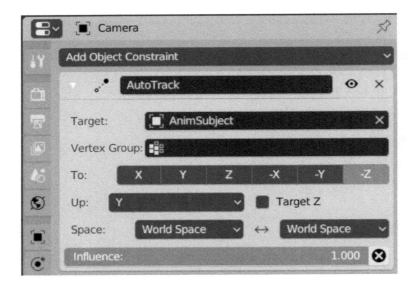

Figure 8.1 - *Track To Constratint*

The settings for the constraint in a camera will need you to specify the target object that your camera will follow, and also the axis used for tracking:

– **To**: Use the -Z option to make your camera look to the object.
– **Up**: Here you have to use the Y option to align the camera Y-axis with the world Y-axis. Don't change this option unless you want to rotate the camera.

Now you will have the camera following all movements made by the target object.

8.1.1 Making an object following a path

Besides making the camera follow an object for animation, we can also use a path that will help with complex trajectories. If you try to move objects in animation using lots of curves and turns, you will need a lot of keyframes to make a compelling motion.

By using a curve object in Blender, we can make any object use that curve as a path for animations. You can create curve objects using the SHIFT+A keys and go to the Curve group (Figure 8.2).

Figure 8.2 - *Curve objects*

From the curve object list, you will see that we can create two types of objects:

– **Bezier**: A curve that will feature points control handlers.

245

– **Circle**: A curve that also has points and control handlers, but already in a circle shape.

Using the Circle option will enable you to create circular trajectories for animation. If you make the camera to follow that circle and use a Track To constraint, you will be able to create an animation called "Turntable." In that animation, a camera will fly around an object in a circular trajectory.

To create that type of animation:

1. Create the Circle from the Curve group.

2. Adjust the scale and Z coordinate of your curve with the S and G keys.

3. Select the camera first, and holding the SHIFT key, add the circle to the selection.

4. Press the CTRL+P keys and choose "Follow Path."

5. Select the camera only and got o the **Object → Clear → Origin** menu. That will make the camera origin to align with the circle.

6. Select the camera and holding the SHIFT key add the object you want to stay at the center of your circle to the selection.

7. Go to the **Object → Track → Track To Constraint** menu.

If you press the SPACEBAR, you will see the camera following the circle as a path for the animation.

Tip: Use an Empty as the target for your camera to follow. That way you will have more flexibility to move the focus point for your animation.

By default, your follow path animation will always have 100 frames in length. You can change that by selecting the circle and opening the Object Data tab. There you will find a field called Path Animation (Figure 8.3).

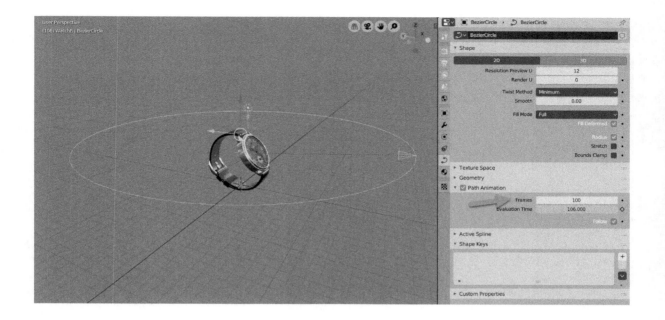

Figure 8.3 - *Path Animation*

Change the Frames option to the amount you want to use for the animation. To break the Follow Path animation, you can select the object that is following the curve and press ALT+P. Choose the "Clear Parent" option, and the object will stop following the curve.

Tip: Be careful not to create a Circle from the Mesh group instead of the Curve. The circle from the Mesh group doesn't support the Follow Path animation.

8.2 Creating animation loops

Animation in Blender will work in a linear way where you will define a start and end frames for them to happen. However, using a special feature of the Graph Editor, it is possible to make any motion to loop forever or with a defined number of repetitions.

To make an animation loop, you will have to create the motion first and keep in mind that it must be ready for the loop. For instance, if you want to make an object go back and forward forever, you should work in a way that your last frame uses the same property from the first.

An excellent way to make animations that shares the first and last positions in the same keyframe is to add all keyframes before applying any motion. In Figure 8.4, we have an object that we can animate by making it scale up and down.

Figure 8.4 - *Object for animation*

The animation will have 1.5 seconds with 30 FPS, which means we will use 45 frames. Here is the animation breakdown:

- **Frame 1**: Object will have a scale factor of 1
- **Frame 22**: Object will have a scale factor of 1.5
- **Frame 45**: Object will have a scale factor of 1

Add keyframes with the scale type for frames 1, 22, and 45 with the object selected. Since you didn't apply any scale transformation, the keyframes will have a scale factor of 1.

Go to frame 22 and apply a scale to the object with a factor of 1.5 by:

1. Pressing the S key
2. Type 1.5
3. Press RETURN to confirm

Part of the trick of using animation loops is that you should skip the last frame. At the animation settings, you should make the Start and End frames as 1 and 44. Why not 45 for the End frame?

The reason to use 44 is simple: you want to avoid having two consecutive frames using a scale factor of 1. If you use frame 45 as the End, you will have frame 45, and 1 played in sequence. It will create a quick stop for your animation and break the fluidness of motion.

8.2.1 Using modifiers in the Graph Editor

With the animation ready, we can create the loop by using modifiers in the Graph Editor. Open the Editor and press the N key to view your Sidebar (Figure 8.5).

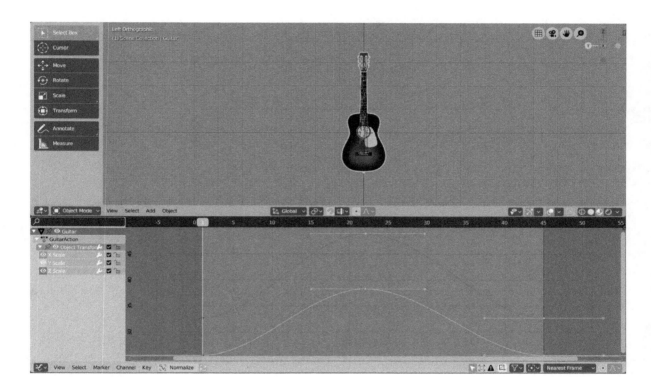

Figure 8.5 - Graph Editor

At the Sidebar, you will open the Modifiers tab and add a Cycles modifier to the curves. That will create an animation loop for your curve. You will immediately see the difference with the curve visualization (Figure 8.6).

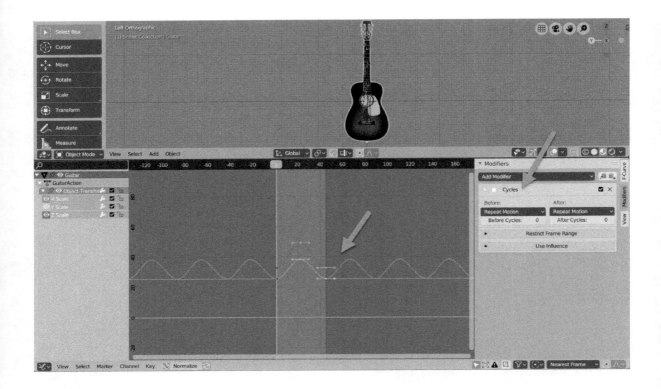

Figure 8.6 - Animation loop

You can control certain aspects of your loop at the Cycles options. In the settings, you will find a Before and After options where you can control the number of repetitions.

By using zero for both settings, you will get the animation repeating forever, or you can pick a number of repetitions to limit your loop. Below you can also restrict the Start and End frames used for the loop.

8.3 Organizing projects in scenes

Each project you work in Blender will feature something called a scene that you can later reference or use for rendering. The scene selector is at the top right of your interface and will always start with the default "scene" (Figure 8.7).

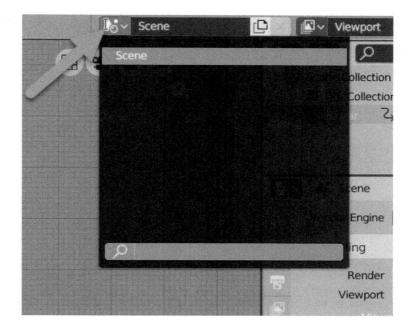

Figure 8.7 - Scene selector

There you can change the current scene and create new scenes based on a few options. If you click at the button to the right of your scene name, you will see the types of scenes you can create (Figure 8.8).

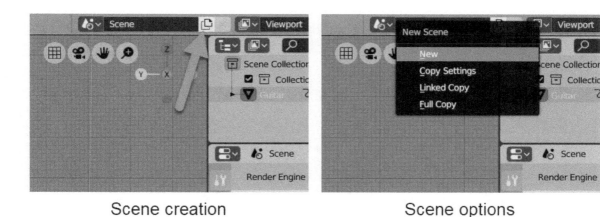

Scene creation   Scene options

Figure 8.8 - Scene creation options

From the options you have:

- **New**: A completely new and independent scene that won't have any objects. An empty new scene.

- **Copy Settings**: An empty new scene that will use some of the settings used from the current scene.

- **Linked copy**: A copy of your current scene that has links to all objects and settings. If you have to create animations with the same objects but using unique types of motion, you can use this option.

- **Full copy**: A copy of your current scene with all models and settings but no links with the original objects.

Besides working as a way to organize large projects in Blender, you can also use scenes to render large projects in sequence. If you use the Video Sequencer Editor later, it will be possible to instance a full scene for animation editing.

8.4 Rendering animation

After you have a full animation with cameras and all the objects ready, it is time to start rendering the project. Unlike a still image where you will handle and see the final result at the Output window, an animation with dozens, hundreds, or thousands of frames will require a dedicated folder to organize the output.

Before we start the process of rendering an animation, you will have to set the output folder for the project in the Output tab (Figure 8.9).

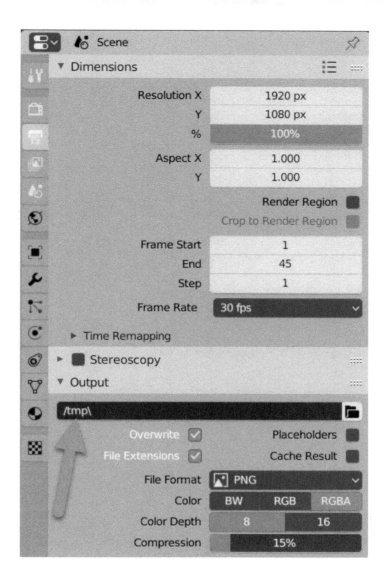

Figure 8.9 - Output folder

There you can locate and set a folder in your computer that will store all frames or video from the animation.

Once you have the output folder for the animation, it will be time to make an important choice regarding animation rendering. You will be able to process your animation as a video file or image sequence:

- **Video file**: You can render the animation in formats like MP4, MKV, or OGG

- **Image sequence**: The animation will appear as a sequence of individual image files like PNG or JPG.

Having your animation rendered as a video file might be convenient for quick visualization. But if you want to have a flexible workflow and avoid the need for rendering everything again, you should use an image sequence.

The most significant benefit of working with an image sequence is that you can keep a lossless version of all your animation frames. By choosing the PNG image format, you can later generate a video file and include titles and effects.

8.4.1 Rendering as a video file

In case you want to use a video file for the animation output, you will have to choose the proper option in the "File Format" field of the Output tab. There you will see three main options for the Movie output:

- AVI JPEG
- AVI Raw
- FFmpeg video

If you want to use modern video containers for your output like MP4, you will choose the FFmpeg video option. With that option, you will see a new panel below called Encoding (Figure 8.10).

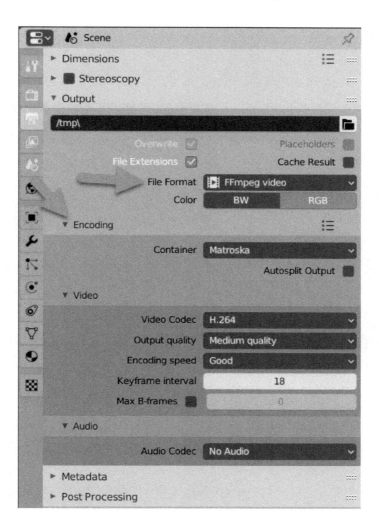

Figure 8.10 - *Video output*

At the Encoding options, you will be able to choose several options to create the MP4 file or any other format you wish to use for your animation. A quick way to set up all options for the video file is with the use of existing presets in Blender (Figure 8.11).

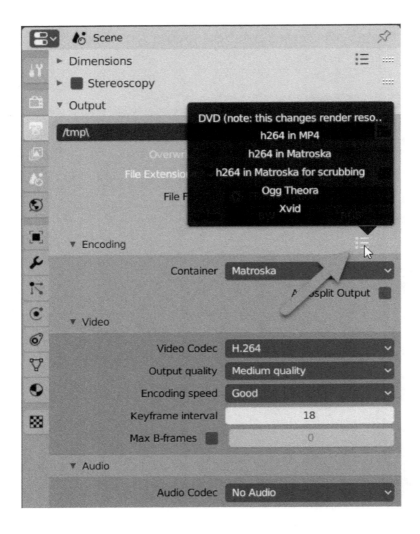

Figure 8.11 - *Video presets*

One of the presets has "h264 in MP4" that already has all the options ready to create such file. You might want to change a few details about the video. For instance, you can change the Output quality from "Medium quality" to "High quality" or Lossless.

That will keep your video file with the highest quality and generate a large file in size. In the audio field, you will notice that it will show an option "No audio." Because the frames of our animation from the 3D Viewport doesn't feature any audio, you should keep the option as "No audio" (Figure 8.12).

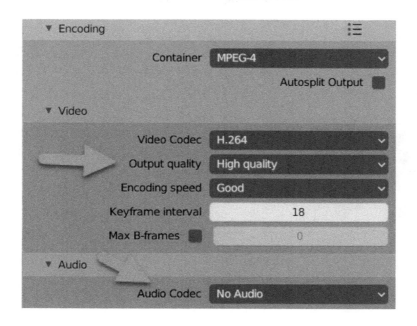

Figure 8.12 - Video encoding

You will be able to add audio for any animation later in the Video Sequencer Editor and use those settings to control both format and quality for any audio data.

After you have all settings in place, it is time to start rendering the animation. You can press CTRL+F12 or go to the **Render → Render Animation** menu. The rendering of animation will most likely take a long time, and you should prepare the computer to stay processing the project for a while.

For projects using Cycles for rendering the animation might require a couple of hours or days to process the animation. You can have an idea about how long it will take by making a quick calculation.

If one frame takes in average 1 minute to render and the full length of your animation has 2400 frames, it will take 2400 minutes (1-minute x 2400) to finish. That will roughly give 40 hours of rendering — almost two days of processing the animation.

Once the process comes to an end, you will see the file created in the Output folder (Figure 8.13).

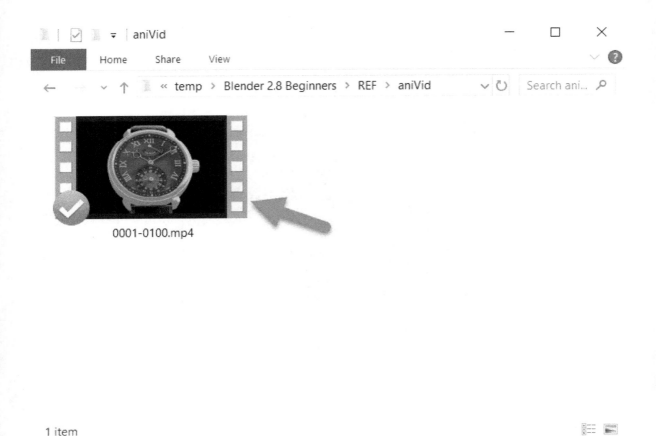

Figure 8.13 - Video saved in the Output folder

The same applies for an image sequence, but instead of a single file, you will see one image file for each one of the frames.

Info: Another benefit of rendering animations as image sequences is that you can start over the process in case of a problem. For instance, if your computer crashes after rendering frame 1000 from 2400, you can come back and start from frame 1001. In a video file, you would have to start from the beginning.

8.5 Editing and exporting video

The rendering of animation to either a video file or image sequence is the starting point of a process that will result in the final version of your project. You will most likely use multiple scenes for the animation or add effects and titles. You can do all that inside Blender without the need for any external resources.

One of the editors from Blender can handle and manipulate video files and works like a non-linear video editor. With the Video Sequencer Editor, you can do all that and much more.

To use the editor, you can use any available space from the interface or open a dedicated WorkSpace for video editing. The WorkSpace is the best choice because it already offers all the options to edit and process video comfortably.

From the WorkSpace selector, you can choose **Video Editing** → **Video Editing** to open an interface that has all editors ready for the task (Figure 8.14).

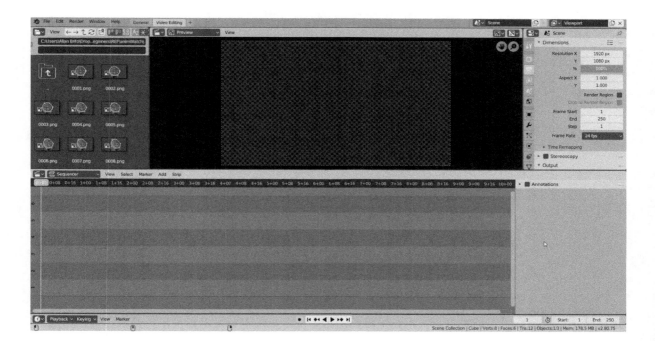

Figure 8.14 - *Video Editing WorkSpace*

At the bottom, you will see the Video Sequencer Editor with all the channels that can receive tracks with video, audio, and image sequences. At the top you have another Video Sequencer Editor, but with the Preview mode active. That will show a preview of all your strips.

To the right, you have the rendering output settings and a file browser on the left.

You can add content to the editor using the Add menu and choose from video files (Movie), Audio files (Sound), or Image/Sequence (Figure 8.15).

Figure 8.15 - Add menu

For instance, we can select the Image/Sequence option and select all files from a sequence with the A key. They will appear in the sequencer as a block of content called strip (Figure 8.16).

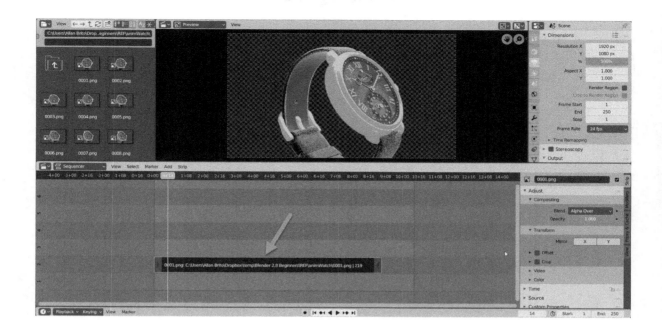

Figure 8.16 - Image sequence as a track

It will be possible to manipulate the video strip, using the same shortcuts to select and move objects. At the borders of the strip, you will also see a small triangle at the beginning and end. You can click to select those triangles and using the G key contract or expand the strip.

If you used the transparent option for rendering PNG files as a sequence, you would be able to compose it with a background. Each channel works as a layer with the lower strips appearing in the back. Placing a still image at the bottom of your channels will make it appear in the back (Figure 8.17).

Figure 8.17 - Image in the back

The transparency only appears because we have a composition mode selected in the Sidebar of your Sequencer. There you can choose a Strip a choose Alpha Over (Figure 8.18).

Figure 8.18 - Alpha Over effect

There are other Compositing modes available, but only with the Alpha Over we will be able to use the transparent background from the image sequence. At the bottom, you also have an Opacity control to make a Strip transparent.

Tip: You can add keyframes to any property in the Sequencer Sidebar.

8.5.1 Editing video

With the Video Sequencer Editor, you have all the tools and options from a traditional video editor. For instance, you can cut strips to remove or reorder parts of your animation. To cut a video, you will use the K key with a strip selected (Figure 8.19).

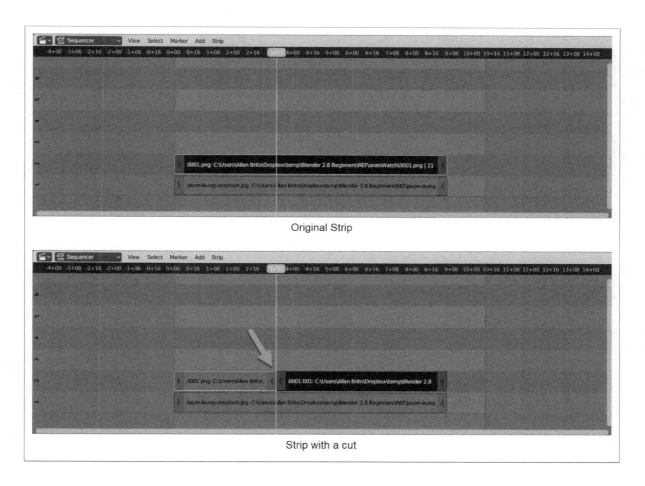

Figure 8.19 - *Cutting a strip*

After you cut a strip, it will be possible to select each part and reorder the video for exporting.

It is not possible to join two different strips, but you can make something called a MetaStrip. That is a composed strip made from several parts. You will create a MetaStrip by selecting multiple strips and pressing the CTRL+G key (Figure 8.20).

263

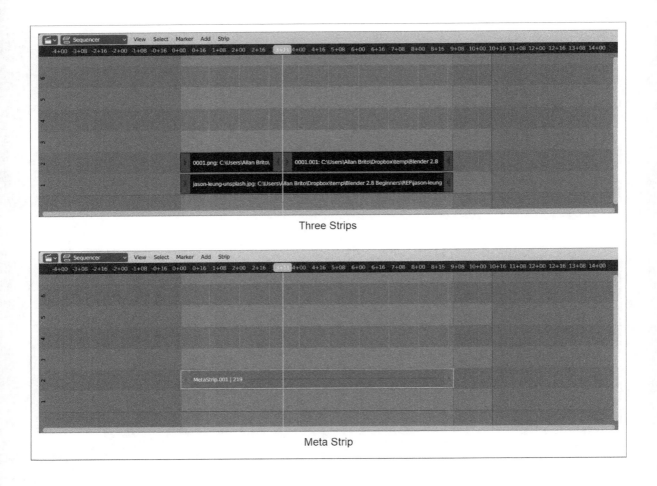

Figure 8.20 - MetaStrip

If you select a MetaStrip and press the TAB key, you will be able to edit the contents of that block.

8.5.2 Exporting video

Once you add any content to the Video Sequencer Editor, all the rendering from Blender will start using the contents from the Editor. The reason for that is because you will have an option enabled at the Post Processing field at the Render tab. There you will find the "Sequencer" option enabled (Figure 8.21).

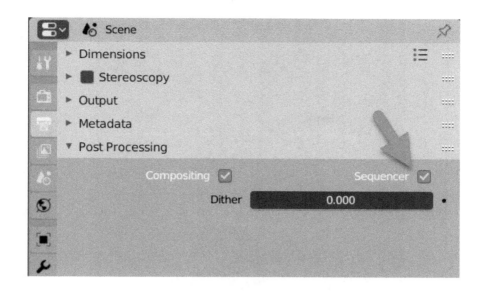

Figure 8.21 - *Sequencer option*

Unless you disable the Sequencer, it will be a matter of using the CTRL+F12 keys to render a video from the Sequencer. Make sure you choose the proper settings in the Output options to create a video file.

That is the moment where you can convert an image sequence to a video file, and also include sounds. From the Add menu in the Sequencer, you can include Sound strips to the project.

Rendering a video from the Sequencer will be much faster than generating all the content from 3D objects. Since you already processed the 3D content, it will be a matter of converting all the effects and images to video.

8.6 Adding titles and text

Most animation projects will also need some titles in the video to display information before or after the content. That could help you to add credits to the project or a simple title.

To add text to any video in the Sequencer, you will use the Add menu and choose the Text option (Figure 8.22).

Figure 8.22 - Text for video

The text will appear as a separate Strip that you can edit by selecting it from the Sequencer and going to the Sidebar. There you will find options to change details like the font and also the text appearing in the Strip (Figure 8.23).

Figure 8.23 - *Text detais*

Add as many text Strips you need for your project and once you have all the required information for a project, press the CTRL+F12 keys to start rendering your video.

What is next?

You know have a solid base to create lots of different types of projects in Blender from 3D modeling, rendering, and animation. The next step now is to get some ideas for projects regarding visualization and animation to practice.

In the first projects, you will probably find some speed bumps and problems. But with a little patience and the help of our book, you will find most solutions for any projects.

Don't miss the opportunity to develop even more your skills with Blender. Only with personal projects, you will be able to take the next step and start migrating to more complex projects with:

- Character animation

- Advanced rendering

- Visual FX

- Advertising creation

- Architectural visualization

- Product design

- Game Development

Blender can help you with all those projects, and all you need is to focus your projects on a particular subject. Then you will start acquiring experience in each one of those fields.

CPSIA information can be obtained
at www.ICGtesting.com
Printed in the USA
LVHW100957110420
653071LV00026B/2752